To "Big" Ken Josper(?)

Best wishes

[signature] 5/95

Victims

A Survival Guide
for the Age of Crime

ISBN 0-9632355-1-6

——

This book is based on reports of actual crimes. However, some events and character dialogue have been altered or fictionalized for dramatic effect. Also, names, dates, locations, and events have been changed to protect the privacy of victims and their families. Any similarities between the characters portrayed herein and any person, living or dead, is purely coincidental.

——

Crime prevention techniques cited in this book were obtained from various outside sources, including, but not limited to, federal, state and local law enforcement officials and crime prevention experts. We believe the information to be accurate and reliable. However, we do not warrant the accuracy or reliability of the information contained herein. Furthermore, Guardian Press makes no guarantees of results from the use of information contained herein. We assume no liability in connection with either the information contained in this book or the crime prevention suggestions made. Moreover, we would caution that it cannot be assumed that every acceptable crime prevention procedure is contained in this book. Obviously, abnormal, unusual or individual circumstances may require further or additional procedures.

Published by Guardian Press
10924 Grant Road #225
Houston, TX 77070

Victims

A Survival Guide
for the Age of Crime

By Richard L. Bloom

We enact many laws that manufacture criminals, and then a few that punish them.

Tucker—*Instead of a Book*

My objective all sublime I shall achieve in time— To let the punishment fit the crime.

W.S. Gilbert—*Mikado*

Contents

The crimes recounted in the following stories all occurred in one 24-hour period across America. The date itself is not important. It was just another typical day in the age of crime.

Preface

Each year, I conduct hundreds of personal safety seminars involving thousands of people. I'm continually amazed at the number of people who think crime is something that only happens to other people. Like the ostrich with his head in the sand, they seem to think, "If I don't see it, it won't bother me."

Every morning we read in our newspapers about the rapes, muggings and murders of the previous day. The evening news gives us more news, complete with gory videotape footage, and yet...most people still think it will never happen to them.

Crime is a reality of life, not a pleasant one, but a reality all the same. Bad guys are out there. They usually look for people who are least able to protect themselves: the elderly, the handicapped or the woman with her hands full of packages and a child on each arm. Since most people don't expect it to happen, they have no idea what to do when it actually does. As a result, they usually do the wrong things.

You can lessen your chances of being victimized by making a few changes in your habits. Simple things like learning to be aware of what's going on around you, being observant of potentially dangerous situations. I suggest role playing with other family members involving different situations. That way, if something ever does happen, you would have a reflex plan rather than just panic. Most importantly, give yourself the benefit of the doubt. Don't worry about offending someone or doing something foolish (like screaming) if you feel threatened. Being foolish is better than being dead.

The following stories are not intended to frighten you into becoming a recluse, but rather to enlighten you about the sad realities that plague honest, law-abiding citizens. The victims in these stories probably thought it would never happen to them. The ones who survived know better. So do the families of the victims. Every victim is somebody's mother, father, sister, brother, son or daughter. Their grief will last a lifetime.

Richard L. Bloom
Crime Deterrent Specialist

Introduction

Crime in America has gone far beyond the epidemic stage. It is now a pandemic plague in this country, and if it continues to grow and spread at its present rate, it threatens to destroy our society as we know it today.

Crime has already caused many Americans to make drastic changes in their lives. The days when we could peacefully enjoy the sanctity of our homes, with windows raised and doors left unlocked through the night, now seem like ancient history. Our homes have become virtual fortresses complete with sophisticated alarm systems, burglar bars and multiple locks on doors and windows.

Instead of settling in for a quiet evening at home, many Americans now hunker down for the siege, with guns and other defensive weapons at the ready.

And venturing out away from our homes has almost turned into a game of Russian roulette. Something as innocent as stopping at a convenience store for a loaf of bread can get you killed.

Trust and caring have been replaced by suspicion and a "don't get involved" attitude. We try to avoid contact with strangers, even eye contact, for the wrong kind of look on our faces could get us killed.

The stories that follow are about real people who became victims of violent crime in one 24-hour period in America. They represent just a few of the thousands of people who are victimized every day in this country. While the victims are real, the names, dates and locations have been changed. None of the stories are strange, bizarre or sensational. Unfortunately, they have become almost commonplace today, so commonplace, in fact, that many of them warrant only a few lines on the back pages of the local newspaper.

We had little trouble finding stories for this book. In fact we could have written several volumes, even though we included none of the myriad crimes committed by street gangs, or the thousands of crimes involving date rape, sexual abuse, incest, or domestic violence.

The stories themselves present a rather septic view of the crimes. We have deliberately omitted most of the gruesome, horrifying details, concentrating instead on providing an overview of the situations and events that led the victims into harm's way. Each crime is then analyzed to help you better understand its causes—and what the victim might have done to avoid it. Specific survival techniques follow each story and analysis.

It truly is a "jungle" out there. The bad guys are the predators; honest, law-abiding citizens are the prey. Each day turns into a test of wile and cunning where only the fittest survive. It is our sincere belief that this book will teach you many of the skills and techniques that can help make you one of the survivors.

12:05 a.m., San Antonio, Texas

Jerry Trent froze as he felt the click of the land mine detonator under his foot. Then he heard the explosion and felt a blinding pain in his left leg as he was hurled through the air, landing in a heap ten feet away. Jerry looked down at the bloody pulp of his left leg and screamed. Just before he lost consciousness, he thought he saw the face of an angel.

In a sense, it was an angel. It was the face of Mike Thornton. Mike Thornton, his inseparable friend from the time they had met after arriving in Vietnam eight months earlier, lifted Jerry onto his back and carried him to an evacuation point nearly two miles away. It wasn't the first time Mike had rescued Jerry, and it wouldn't be the last. Mike had helped Jerry through battles in the field, as well as barroom brawls in Saigon and Da Nang. Jerry had nicknamed him "Iron Mike" because of his toughness and strength.

Five years later, Mike Thornton would come to Jerry's rescue once again. The land mine had blown away part of Jerry's left foot. After nearly two years of surgery, much of his foot had been rebuilt, and although he walked with a limp, he survived the ordeal with his limbs intact. But the emotional scars ran much deeper, and Jerry battled his depression with drugs and alcohol. Mike had intervened to help Jerry work through it. He had even helped Jerry land a job as an outside salesman with Watlen Valve in Denver, Colorado. It was the job Jerry still held nearly 20 years later.

Jerry eventually became a good salesman. Not great, just good. Perhaps that's why he had been passed over numerous times for sales manager that would have landed him a more settled life in the home office. After all these years of busting his butt, he was still spending more than half his life away from home, covering markets in his territory of Texas, Oklahoma and New Mexico.

He lamented that fact as he sipped a maragarita at the bar along the Riverwalk in San Antonio. He had had a lousy trip so far, closing only two small deals in Dallas and one in Austin. San Antonio had been a complete washout. Maybe he'd make up for it in Houston, he thought to himself as he ordered a fresh drink.

Jerry had rented a car in Dallas to make the swing down to Austin and San Antonio and then over to Houston. He had planned to be on the road to Houston by now, but a torrential rainstorm had dumped more than three inches of rain on San Antonio, and the same storm system was moving east toward Houston. He didn't relish making the three-hour drive in a blinding rainstorm, so he had checked into a San Antonio hotel for the night. The rain had stopped so he walked over to the Riverwalk, one of his favorite haunts in the Alamo city.

The Riverwalk consists of restaurants and night clubs built along the San Antonio River that cuts through the center of the city. From his table by the terrace, Jerry watched the people come and go as he sipped his drink. Even at 7:15 p.m. on a stormy day, the Riverwalk was crowded with tourists. He knew he should eat something, but he really wasn't hungry. Besides, he was too bummed out to eat. No, he'd just sit there, drown his concerns and watch the people come and go.

By 11:45, Jerry's problems seemed to have disappeared in a sea of margaritas. But his problems were just beginning. Jerry had gotten into the swing of things with the Mexican band that had come on at 9:00 to liven the place up. He had put away five more margaritas and was now totally sloshed. He figured it was about time to get back to his hotel—if he could find it, he chuckled to himself.

When the waitress brought his tab 10 minutes later, Jerry drunkenly pulled out a large wad of bills, and with the help of his waitress, finally managed to count out the money. Lately, Jerry had been carrying mostly cash on his trips. Watlen Valve didn't supply its sales force with credit cards, preferring instead to have each salesman arrange for his own expenses then turn in receipts for reimbursement. Jerry's credit cards had been maxxed out for nearly a year now, so cash was his only option. Travelers' checks were just too much trouble, Jerry thought. Besides, as Jerry liked to say, "Cash makes no enemies." Nobody ever turns you down when you pay with cash.

Jerry started out the door on unsteady legs. He paid no attention to Jody Collins who was paying his tab at the bar as Jerry walked by. He didn't notice that Jody left the bar a few seconds behind him.

Last week at this time, Jody Collins was behind bars at the Beto Unit of the Texas State Penitentiary, doing 25 years for armed robbery of a convenience store two years ago. He was one of thousands of hardened criminals released from Texas prisons by order of Judge W. W. Shafter, a federal judge in Tyler, Texas. Not only were the prisons overcrowded, but the prisoners actually had to do hard labor. Judge Shafter thought that constituted cruel and unusual punishment, so he ordered the state to turn murderers, robbers and rapists out onto the streets of Texas. Jody Collins was one of those early releases. He was supposed to have reported to a halfway house in San Antonio two days earlier. He never made it there.

Instead, he broke into a house 10 miles away and stole a gun and some electronic equipment. He traded the electronic equipment for crack cocaine. But he kept the gun and went looking for easier pickings down on the Riverwalk. He found Jerry Trent.

Jerry knew nothing about Judge Shafter, Jody Collins or the absurdities of the justice system. All Jerry knew was that he hadn't the foggiest idea where his hotel was as he half staggered east along the Riverwalk. On top of that, his bladder was aching, and he direly needed to relieve himself. He came to a walkway that went off to his left through a stand of palm trees and shrubs, beyond which were steps leading up to street level. It looked like as good a place as he was likely to find, so he turned and hurried along the walkway.

He hadn't gone more than 20 feet when he heard the sounds of someone coming up quickly behind him. Under the burden of eight or nine drinks, his reflexes were too slow for him to even turn his head to look. Suddenly, he felt a gun in his back and Jody Collins saying, "Keep your mouth shut and give me your money and you won't get hurt."

"What the hell?" Jerry stammered in slurred speech.

Jody jammed the gun into Jerry's back hard enough to cause him to wince in pain.

"Damn, man, what the hell you doin'?" Jerry yelled, still not fully comprehending what was going on.

Jody then punched Jerry hard at the base of the neck and said through clenched teeth, "Give me the money now, or I'll blow your ass off!"

Jerry suddenly lurched around to face his abductor, and for some reason known only to Jerry, awkwardly lunged for the gun in Jody's hand. Jody fired instinctively, hitting Jerry squarely in the chest, knocking his body back several feet. Even as Jerry was falling backward, Jody was moving forward to quickly rifle his pockets. Still in a daze from the alcohol and the bullet wound in his chest, Jerry looked up through glazed eyes as Jody pulled the wad of bills from his pants pocket and scurried away into the night.

For an instant, Jerry thought he was back in Vietnam. As he lay there gasping for breath, he almost expected to see Mike Thornton appear out of nowhere to lift him up and carry him to safety once again. This time, though, not even Mike Thorton could save him. Jerry took one last gasp at breath, and tried to sit up. A surprised look came over his face as he slumped back and died.

Jerry's murder was the first officially recorded on this particular day in America. Ironically, it came 20 years to the day that he had almost died in Vietnam.

Survival Analysis

Jerry Trent is another needless casualty in the siege of American streets. His death could have easily been avoided. In fact, he died knowing better.

As a veteran not only of the Vietnam war but also years on the road as a salesman, Jerry was aware of all the dangers he faced. But Jerry wasn't too worried. He felt like he could handle himself in almost any situation, even with his physical handicap. He still knew the self-defense techniques he'd learned in hand-to-hand combat drills in the military. As he discovered, though, the streets of America can be just as deadly as the jungles of Vietnam. One careless act is all it takes to get yourself killed.

To say that Jerry acted carelessly is an understatement. Reckless is a better description. But that isn't meant as an indictment. No victim of crime is ever to blame, regardless of how foolish or careless the victim's actions. Jerry was just being human. But he made himself extremely vulnerable by getting drunk. A person who's intoxicated isn't capable of making intelligent decisions. Had Jerry been sober, he probably would not have flashed the roll of bills when he paid his tab at the bar.

He also might have handled the situation differently when he was confronted by the robber. Standing face to face with an armed robber is no time for heroics. Passive compliance with the robber's demands probably would have saved his life.

Had Jerry been in command of his faculties, there are several things he could have done to increase his chances of survival. First of all, he could have let the robber know he would comply without resistance. Jerry should have complied quickly but with cautious motions as he assured the robber that he wasn't armed and that he was only reaching for his money. At the same time, he might have had the presence of mind to slowly inch his body sideways to the robber so as to present less of a target in the event the gun went off. Even the slightest movement can be misinterpreted by a robber, so it's best to explain your actions as you comply—and at the same time, make it harder to be hit in the event the gunman fires. Last and most obvious, he would never have tried to disarm the gunman.

Of course, most sober people would know better than to fight with an armed robber. But Jerry wasn't sober, and now he's dead. It's hard enough to keep from being victimized even with a clear head. With every sip of a drink, you're reducing your ability to make intelligent decisions. When you're face to face with a criminal, nothing is more important than staying calm and in control of your actions.

How to Keep It from Happening to You.

1. Don't drink to the point of intoxication. Whether you're out in public or in your home, having a clear head is essential for dealing with a crisis of any sort. Remember, too, criminals always seek out the easiest victim. They don't come much easier than someone who is drunk.

2. Never flash money in public. Criminals like nothing better than cash. The more money you have on you, the greater risk a robber will take to get it from you.

3. Don't be lulled into a false sense of security by your circumstances or surroundings. Many men have the mistaken notion that robbers and muggers target mainly women as their victims. A desperate criminal, especially one who is armed, will take on even the most formidable looking man under the right circumstances. Also, just because you're in a well-lighted, well-traveled part of town, don't lower your guard.

4. Be aware of what's going on around you at all times, particularly when you're out in public. If something or someone looks even slightly suspicious, try to take evasive action. Turn around and walk in the opposite direction, cross the street or step into a store or shop. This day and age, you have to go out of your way to avoid becoming a victim.

5. When you're traveling, be extra alert. You're far more vulnerable when you're in unfamiliar surroundings. Try to stay on "the beaten path" as often as possible to avoid accidently venturing into high crime areas.

6. If you're confronted by a mugger, don't resist. Remember, a lot of the criminals on the street are drug addicts who are desperate for money to feed their habit. They have no compunction about killing to get what they need. It's far better to surrender your possessions than to lose your life.

7. If a robber is holding a gun or knife on you, comply with all demands quickly but cautiously. Don't make any sudden moves. Be deliberate without seeming to stall. Explain every move to the robber before you make it so there's less likelihood of his misinterpreting your actions. Try to maneuver your body into a position that presents a smaller target in the event the robber fires his weapon.

8. Do not try to reason with the robber or talk him out of his actions. The slightest delay in complying with his demands could get you killed. The objective is to get rid of the robber as soon as you can safely do so. The longer it takes for the situation to unfold, the greater your chances of being killed or injured.

1:40 a.m., Albuquerque, New Mexico

D etective David Bryant leaned against the fender of his car and lit another cigarette. The ambulance carrying Amanda Wygant had just departed the scene. After a minute or two, he dropped the half-smoked cigarette and ground it out with his shoe. For the third time in the last 20 minutes, he pulled a small notebook from his coat pocket and flipped the pages over until he reached the notes he had made about Amanda.

The laundry room was covered with splattered blood; he assumed it was the victim's. One washing machine was loaded with clothes, including brown trousers with tan stripes down the outer seams, the pants to her Albuquerque, New Mexico, police uniform. No dryers had been used. Amanda was evidently waiting for her clothes to finish washing when the assailant had entered the scene. Even though it was in the low forties, Amanda was wearing only a housecoat. She had struggled with her assailant, as the epidermal tissue under her fingernails seemed to indicate. She had also been brutally raped.

Amanda Wygant had been found by Chester Irving, a maintenance man just home from work who needed to do his laundry. Mr. Irving reported the lights in the laundry room were off when he entered, which was unusual according to the apartment manager. Turning on the lights, he spotted her slumped on the floor immediately adjacent to the washing machines.

Bryant looked up from his notebook. Amanda had probably been pushed over one of the machines, her stomach resting on the closed lid and her feet touching the floor, housecoat ripped off, and raped. Bryant returned to his notes.

She must have been caught completely by surprise. Her .38 revolver still lay in the pink plastic laundry basket. The assailant could have been waiting for her or someone else to enter the laundry room, possibly hiding in the small closet next to the door. Amanda had been beaten severely about the head. It appeared that her jaw and cheek bones as well as her nose were broken. Clumps of hair were widely strewn on the floor. Amanda must have put up a real fight, Bryant thought to himself.

Amanda Wygant stood five-foot eight and carried 142 pounds on her "big-boned" frame. She had long, flaming red hair that she always wore in a bun while on duty. She worked out in the gym three nights a week, placing heavy emphasis on weights. She probably gave a good account of herself in the fight. Her attacker was probably licking his own wounds, Bryant thought.

The watch Amanda was wearing had apparently been smashed in the fight. It had stopped at exactly 1:40, giving Willis at least an indication of the time of the attack. Mr. Irving had discovered her in the laundry room nearly three hours later. "Why in the hell was she down here at one o'clock in the morning washing her clothes?" Bryant wondered to himself. You'd think she had seen enough of these things to know better, he thought. She must have figured she had enough protection with the .38 along. It didn't do her much good laying in the laundry basket, though. The assailant must not have seen it, otherwise he'd probably have taken it with him when he left.

Bryant had already checked out Amanda's apartment and found nothing that indicated foul play. In all likelihood, her attacker was either someone out for revenge, possibly for some prior arrest Amanda had made, or simply some nut prowling the apartment complex looking for easy prey. He would definitely give her arrest reports a thorough going over for any leads.

Judging from the skin under her nails and the hair on the floor of the laundry room, Bryant figured her attacker was a white male, apparently fairly strong since he was able to overpower Amanda. The lab crew was still in the laundry room taking prints from the washing machines, the light switch, the closet door knob and the door of a dryer that was found open. Hopefully, they would have something for him in a couple of hours that might help identify her assailant. Mr. Irving had been fingerprinted as a routine procedure to eliminate his prints from any others found at the scene.

Bryant had just lit another cigarette when the call came over the police radio. Amanda Wygant had died on the way to the hospital.

Bryant closed his notebook and walked back inside the laundry room. The lab crew was gathering up the evidence they had collected when Bryant stepped in and said, "Make sure you get everything. We've got a homicide on our hands. She died en route to the hospital." No one said a word. They just shook their heads in disbelief. How could something like this happen to one of their own?

David Bryant got in his car and headed for home. He'd try to get a few hours of sleep. It was going to be a long day.

Survival Analysis

Amanda Wygant's case is a classic example of a victim thinking, "It can't happen to me." There she was, an experienced police officer well trained in the art of self-defense, armed with a revolver. Yet she was attacked, brutalized and murdered in the apartment complex where she lived. If it can happen to Amanda Wygant, it can surely happen to any one of us—at almost any time of the day or night.

The fact that it happened to Amanda around 1:40 a.m. in a deserted laundry room at her apartment complex points up the dangers of becoming too confident of our ability to defend ourselves. Most of us are no match for a desperate criminal who has the element of surprise on his side. But then, none of us truly believe it will happen to us in the first place.

Amanda Wygant certainly didn't. In fact, she once boasted to a fellow officer that she hoped some creep would attack her. "It would be the last time that son-of-a-bitch attacked anybody. I'd blow his low-life head off," she told the officer as she patted the trusty .38 revolver in her holster. Amanda certainly felt confident of her abilities. Too confident.

To begin with, she should never have ventured to the laundry room alone in the late night hours. The fact that she was armed made little difference, because the gun was in her laundry basket. About the only way the gun would have helped was if she had been carrying it in her hand. But that would be awkward, cumbersome and downright dangerous.

A small canister of a powerful chemical spray like The Protector might have afforded greater protection. This is a military-grade chemical protection that can stop an attacker from 15 feet away. Amanda could easily have carried a personal-size spray in the palm of her hand, even while holding a laundry basket. Had she been on the alert as she well should have been, she would never have let the spray out of her hand the entire time. When the assailant attacked her, one quick shot from the spray would have stopped him cold. And Amanda would be alive today, telling her story in person rather than having it pieced together by conjecture by a fellow officer investigating her murder.

It is a sad state of affairs when we can't leave our homes without fearing for our lives. But we can't. We simply have to be on the alert, almost to the point of expecting an attack, every time we walk out the door. Sadly, that may be our best defense. It's difficult for a criminal to get the upper hand on a person who is expecting an attack and, thus, has already planned a defense.

We don't mean to suggest that people should be paranoid, just cautious. That may involve changing some habits, even making an attitude adjustment. Amanda Wygant is tragic proof that it can happen to anyone.

How to Keep It from Happening to You.

1. Never assume it can't happen to you. A false sense of security can lead you into great danger. Stay alert to what is happening around you at all times.

2. If you live in an apartment complex, never go to the laundry room alone at night. (Be cautious about it even during the day.) Have someone accompany you. And carry a high-grade chemical spray like The Protector with you for personal protection day and night.

3. Don't take out the garbage at night. Most trash dumpsters are located in alleys or remote areas of an apartment complex, places you don't want to be at night.

4. Be cautious at apartment security gates. Many access gates require you to stop and roll down your car window to enter a code number. Do it as quickly as possible then roll the window back up. As you enter the gate, watch your rear view mirror for anyone running through the open gate behind you.

5. If you have to come and go at night, be on guard when walking from your car to your apartment.

6. Always have your chemical spray canister in the palm of your hand ready to fire. If someone approaches you in a threatening manner, forcefully yell, "Back off!", as you aim The Protector at the person's face. If the person continues toward you in a threatening manner, fire the chemical spray. The powerful fumes from The Protector will quickly subdue the attacker. Leave the scene immediately and go to a safe place to call the police.

2:15 a.m., Memphis, Tennessee

Linda Levisay tensed as she felt the engine sputter on her '84 Toyota. It was 2:15 a.m., and the Loop 240 Freeway on the south side of Memphis was nearly deserted. She had been meaning to get the car checked out for the last month or so, but as a divorcee with two small children, there was barely enough money for food and clothing, let alone car repairs. Working as a cocktail waitress at the Memphis International Airport was the best paying job she could find, but she always worried about having to drive home late at night. As luck would have it, she had plenty to be worried about.

"Oh, Lord," she thought to herself, "Please don't stall out now." Just to be on the safe side, she moved into the lane nearest the shoulder. The car sputtered again. "Damn, why didn't I get this thing fixed?"

The sputtering worsened, and the engine began to backfire as the car strained to ascend an overpass. Realizing that the car wouldn't make it up the incline, Linda pulled onto the shoulder as the car coasted to a stop. "Damn, damn, damn," she screamed as she pounded on the steering wheel in anger. Then she slumped forward on the steering wheel and began to cry, as much in frustration as in fear.

After a few minutes, her sobbing subsided. She nervously lit a cigarette and began weighing her options. She could wait in the car until daylight, then try to get help. Or she could flag down a car. "Maybe a cop will come along," she thought to herself. "No, they're never around when you really need them." Maybe her mother, with whom she lived, would get worried and call someone to come looking for her. Doubtful, though. Her mother was usually sound asleep when Linda came home at night.

Just then, she saw the lights of a car coming up behind her on the nearly deserted freeway. She thought about trying to flag it down, but let it go by. Several other cars zipped by, and she was tempted to try to get the driver's attention, but hesitated each time. Her desperation increased with each passing car. "What the hell am I gonna do?" she muttered to herself. "I can't just sit here all night. I've gotta do something," she thought.

She saw another vehicle approaching and started to wave it down, but once again, caution got the better of her. This time, though, the vehicle slowed down and pulled to a stop along the shoulder a couple of hundred yards ahead. As the vehicle backed down the shoulder toward her, Linda could see that it was a pickup truck. When it stopped in front of her, she was relieved to see what appeared to be a man and a woman in the truck. Her relief would be short lived.

The driver of the truck was Johnny McCombs, a petty thief and pool hustler who had been in trouble with the law almost constantly since the age of 12. Johnny had been cursed with

severe acne in his youth, and his face still showed the ravages of
it some 20 years later. The only redeeming quality Johnny
seemed to have was his long blond hair which he wore at shoulder length. From the back and in the dim light along the freeway,
it was easy for Linda to mistake him for a woman. But Johnny
was the least of Linda's worries.

Skeet Miller who was riding shotgun in the pick-up lived
every minute of his life right on the edge. He had spent 10 of his
29 years in prison in Indiana and Arkansas for armed robbery and
burglary, and was currently wanted as a murder suspect in
Kentucky. Until a broken hip and an insatiable appetite for Jack
Daniels sidelined him, Skeet had been a bull rider on the rodeo
circuit 10 years ago. He still walked with a slight limp, a fact
Linda noted when he stepped out of the truck and approached her
car.

Skeet and Johnny had closed down Poor Devil's Lounge less
than 10 minutes earlier, and Skeet was a little wobbly on his feet
as he smiled and greeted Linda.

"You need some help, mam?" Skeet inquired with feigned
courtesy.

Linda, whose door was locked, cracked her window slightly
and replied, "My car stalled out on me."

Skeet held his hand up to his ear and said, "I can't hear you.
Do you need some help?"

At that, Linda rolled down her window halfway and repeated,
"My car stalled out on me. Could you call a wrecker for me?"

"Well, first let's see if we can get it started. Why dontcha pop
the hood and let me take a look. I'm pretty good with cars."

Thinking of the possibility of saving $50 or so on a wrecker,
Linda gladly complied. She pulled the inside hood release, and
Skeet stepped around and popped it open. After a couple of
minutes of squinting in the darkness under the hood, Skeet

stepped around to the window and said, "I think it's just the distributor cap come loose. You got a screwdriver with you?"

"I'm not sure. There might be one in the trunk," Linda replied with her head sticking partway out the window. She had rolled it down further as she dropped her guard little by little at Skeet's seeming concern. She wasn't quite sure about him, though. He looked harmless enough, but she thought she could smell liquor on his breath. So what, she thought. He and his wife had been out partying, much like she and her ex-husband had done not too many years ago. Besides, there was still some traffic on the freeway in spite of the late hour, and this guy wouldn't try anything here. It never occurred to her that Skeet couldn't possibly have detected the problem with her car given the lighting conditions at the time.

"Open the trunk and let's if it's there," Skeet said as he stepped up to her window.

Linda hesitated. "I'm not sure I have one," she said. "You don't have one with you?"

"No I don't," Skeet replied as if losing his patience. "Look, if you don't want me to help, I'll get in the truck and go call you a wrecker. I was just trying to save you a tow, that's all." He turned and started to leave.

"No, wait. I may have one in the trunk," Linda said. She took the keys from the ignition and stepped out of the car. Skeet followed her to the back of the car. She fumbled to open the trunk and bent over and felt around for the small tool box her ex-husband had kept in the car.

Linda froze when she heard the click of the switchblade knife. In one swift motion, Skeet's left arm was around her neck and the knife in his right hand was at her throat. Suddenly, everything seemed to go into slow motion. The realization of her situation swept over her, the danger she was in, the possibility she

would not survive beyond this moment. It was almost like going
into shock as her body seemed to instantly shut down her defenses and surrender to the point of the knife.

"Whatta ya say we skip the screwdriver and just have a
screw," Skeet whispered in her ear as he pulled her back from the
trunk. "One peep outta you, lady, and you've had it. Got it?" as
he gave her neck a tight squeeze with his arm.

Skeet slammed the trunk shut with his right hand and forced
her to the truck. Inside the truck, Johnny reached over and
popped open the door.

"Howdy, mam," Johnny giggled at the quivering woman who
was shoved onto the seat beside him. Skeet quickly jumped in
behind her and resumed the choke-hold on her neck. "Damned if
you don't look good enough to eat, which I might just do if
you're real nice to me," Johnny said as he started the truck and
peeled out onto the freeway. He looked around her and said to
Skeet, "I'll say one thing for you pardner, you sure have a way
with the ladies."

"Cold steel does it every time," Skeet replied as he waved the
knife in front of Linda's face.

Linda choked out a loud sob. "Please don't hurt me...I'll do
anything you want...just don't hurt me...I've got kids," she said
through Skeet's choke-hold

"Damn right you will," Skeet replied, "and you're gonna love
every minute of it, right?"

Linda nodded her head in agreement as Skeet pushed the
knife to her throat just to the point of breaking the skin. Skeet
revelled in the power he held over the woman. She was his for
the taking, and he'd make her beg and plead for mercy, even her
life.

"Good girl," Johnny said as he reached over and ripped open
her blouse. "Let's see what kind of goodies we got here."

"Damn, you got a pair, don't you," Skeet said as he ripped away her bra. He began roughly squeezing her breasts. "A little foreplay," he said to Johnny with a laugh. "Yessir, I'm not the kind of guy that just jumps on and bangs away without a little warm-up first."

Linda gasped in pain and began shivering, both from fear and the cool night air that rushed over her exposed breasts and shoulders. At that point, Linda seemed to mentally black out.

The rest of the night came to her in surreal, strobe-like flashes of consciousness. She remembered being dragged out of the truck by her hair. Total darkness. Cool, damp air...must be near a river or lake. As her mind drifted in and out of consciousness, she remembered the stillness of the night, the sound of the cicada's droning their nightly songs, the heavy breathing and rough voices of the two men who took turns on top of her, ravaging her body there in thc night, while she lay passively, helplessly on the cold bed of the pick-up truck.

Her body gave only a slight jolt as the knife plunged into her throat the first time. After the third stab, she was dead. Skeet wouldn't stop, however, until he had rammed the knife into her body more that 40 times.

The next day, the police found Linda's car abandoned on the freeway. It would be two years later before her decomposed body was found in the brush along the bank of the Wolf River just outside Memphis.

Johnny McCombs was arrested for her murder after an informant tipped police that Johnny had once bragged about watching a man stab a woman to death. He turned state's evidence against Skeet, and took a plea bargain sentence of 25 years in prison.

Skeet Miller was charged with murder but is still at large.

Survival Analysis

Linda Levisay might be alive today if she had followed her basic instincts. She was leery of trying to flag down a passing car, as well she should have been. She was even cautious enough to remain in her car with the doors locked and the windows rolled up when Skeet first approached her vehicle. She should never have lowered her guard. Once she stepped out of the car, Linda was completely vulnerable.

Linda was mistaken to assume that there was a man and a woman in the pick-up. There wasn't much light on the roadway, and she couldn't really be sure that the driver was a woman. And even if there had been a woman driving the truck, it shouldn't have made a difference to Linda. She should have remained in the locked car with her windows rolled up!

But Linda's first big mistake was in not keeping her car in good working condition. She knew the dangers of being out alone late at night. She also knew that the car had a problem. Had Linda taken proper care of her car, she might be alive today. This is not to say that Linda was to blame. A victim is never to blame for a crime. It is cited here merely to point out the importance of reducing the risk of being stranded on the road to avoid being at the mercy of a stranger's help.

Linda's second big mistake was in not having an emergency plan in the event of car trouble. Here again, this is not meant to blame the victim. But everyone who ventures out on the road should know exactly what to do in case of a car problem. Cars are, after all, imperfect machines that could fail at any time.

How could Linda have planned for an emergency? First and foremost, she should have used the "buddy system." In this case, her mother could have been her buddy. Had she known to expect

Linda home by a certain hour each night, her mother would have known something was wrong when Linda didn't arrive at the stipulated time. Also, Linda should have let her mother know the exact route she traveled to and from work so that someone would know where to find her to provide assistance. With such a plan in place, Linda could have remained in her car, safe in the knowledge that help would soon arrive.

Of course, if Linda had had a cellular phone in her car, she could have called for assistance. Given her financial situation, however, it is understandable that she didn't have a car phone. But for anyone who has to be on the road alone at night—particularly a woman—a car phone should be a priority item in any budget. A cellular phone, combined with membership in an automobile club that provides 24-hour emergency service is excellent insurance for any motorist, man or woman.

Another thing Linda should have had in her car was a fold out sign that read, "Need Assistance. Call the Police." These signs are very inexpensive and usually fold down small enough to easily store inside the car.

Linda also should have had three or four envelopes, each containing a quarter or two and emergency phone numbers. If someone stopped to render aid, she could have passed an envelope through the cracked window then asked the person to go to a phone and call one of the numbers.

Another thing Linda should have had with her was a self-defense weapon, especially since she had to be out alone late at night. But what kind of weapon? It's illegal to carry a concealed weapon in the state of Tennessee (just as it is in most states). And would she have been able to use it? Maybe. But remember, Linda had small children. Guns are extremely dangerous with kids around. Of course, Linda, like so many victims, simply didn't think she would ever need a gun or any other type of defensive weapon. She didn't think it could happen to her.

Had she been more aware of the danger she faced each night, she might have had a canister of high-grade chemical protection spray with her. That way, she could have defended herself had Skeet tried to force his way into her car. As it turned out, though, Skeet had little trouble abducting Linda, because she violated the cardinal rule of a stranded motorist: Stay in your locked car until the police arrive or until someone you know arrives. Once you get out of your car in the presence of a stranger, anything can happen.

The minute Skeet put the knife to her throat, Linda had little choice but to comply with his demands. When an attack reaches this point, there is little anyone can do except go along with the assailant's demands. One of the few options open to Linda at this point was to pretend to faint and become dead weight to Skeet. However, she might have been cut or stabbed by the knife at her throat, so this action was not without a high degree of risk. She also might have released her bladder or bowels, making herself a much less desirable target. But everything happened so quickly. Linda had less than 30 seconds to do anything before she was forced into the truck between the two men. At that point, her situation was virtually hopeless. Or was it?

None of us can say for sure how we'd react in Linda's situation. Linda went into something akin to shock. Her brain seemed to click off, possibly as a way to shut out the terror. Had she been able to maintain her thought processes, there is a very slim chance that she might have escaped. But even a slim chance is better than none. The night was pitch dark. Who knows? There might have been one brief moment when her captors let down their guard. Had she been in command of her faculties, she might have been able to capitalize on the situation and bolt into the darkness. It's doubtful that visibility was greater than ten feet ahead. She just might have escaped and lived to tell about it.

We say again, however, that Linda was not to blame for any of her actions. She did the best she was capable of doing under the circumstances. Why she was killed that night is anyone's guess. She complied with everything she was told to do. She didn't struggle or try to resist. Yet she was brutally murdered. Maybe out of fear or panic on the part of her assailants. Maybe Skeet secretly reviled women. Or maybe it was just the ultimate act of power being played out in Skeet's mind. Quite possibly, not even Skeet knows for sure.

How to Keep It from Happening to You.

1. Don't ever think it can't happen to you. The false notion that crime only happens to other people can ultimately get you killed.

2. Keep your car well maintained and in good working order. A little preventive maintenance on your vehicle can help you avoid getting stranded on the road.

3. If your car does break down, try to maneuver to the side of the road that provides the greatest visibility. If it happens at night, try to get your car underneath a street light if at all possible. If the car is at all operable, say in the case of a flat tire, continue to drive slowly along the shoulder or side of the roadway until you reach a safe, well-lighted place where help is available. You might ruin the tire in the process. But a tire can be replaced. Your life can't be.

4. If you're alone in the car, never get out and try to make repairs. Turn on the car's emergency flashers and stay inside

the car with the doors locked until help arrives. Carry a "Call Police" sign in your car, and display it in the front or back window of your car. Don't roll down the window or get out of the car unless the person who stops to offer help is a policeman or someone you know and trust. If you have to get out of the car to set emergency flares, do it quickly, and get back inside the car as soon as possible, and lock the doors behind you.

5.   In your glove compartment, always have three or four enve-lopes containing emergency phone numbers and several quarters. If a stranger stops to offer help, pass one of the envelopes through a crack in the window, and ask him to go to the nearest phone and call for help. If he means you no harm, he'll understand your reluctance to open the window or get out of the car to talk.

6.   Whenever possible, use the "buddy" system every time you leave home by yourself. Tell your buddy where you're going, the route you'll be taking, the expected time of arrival and the time of your return. When you arrive at your destination, call and let your buddy know. It's also a good idea to call your buddy before you start back home, particularly if you'll be out alone at night. Try not to deviate from your planned schedule or route of travel if at all possible.

7.   If you can possibly afford one, get a cellular phone for your car or purse. If your car breaks down, you can call for help and remain inside your car until help arrives. Make a list of emergency phone numbers and keep it in your car or purse.

8.   Always know the location of safe places along your route. These are places where you can find some degree of protec-tion when you feel threatened. Police stations, fire stations,

all-night drug stores and supermarkets, gas stations, convenience stores and apartment complexes with security guards are good examples of safe places. Obviously, some are safer than others. It's a good idea to make a list of safe places and keep it in your glove compartment.

9. Try to travel well-lighted busy thoroughfares when you go out at night. Avoid taking short-cuts through isolated, unfamiliar parts of town. And just to be on the safe side, try to do as many errands as possible during the daylight hours.

10. Keep a self-defense weapon in your car or purse, but think long and hard before you decide to carry a gun. Remember, it's illegal to conceal a gun in your car or on your person in most states. Also, before you pull a gun on an assailant, be absolutely certain you could shoot to kill. Otherwise, the gun might be taken away and used against you. It's imperative to get professional training on how to use and care for a gun if you decide to carry one. A powerful, high-quality chemical spray such as The Protector is a good alternative to a hand gun. The Protector is a military-grade chemical spray that will incapacitate an assailant for up to 30 minutes without causing permanent physical damage. And it's perfectly legal to carry in most states.

5:40 a.m., San Diego, California

Jogging wasn't merely exercise to Holly Leyendecker. It was a jealous lover, demanding more and more of her time every week. And every day, she succumbed to its call in the early morning hours along the San Diego roadways. Holly thought parks and jogging trails were too dangerous before daylight, so she had mapped a route that took her along well-lighted streets and thoroughfares. Early in the morning, there usually wasn't much traffic. Occasionally, some jerk would whistle or yell something sexual, but Holly paid little attention to such nonsense. She was too busy improving on her nine minute a mile pace. It was this dedication that shortened, rather than extended, her life.

On the morning of her death, Holly had awakened at 5:05, before the alarm went off at the usual 5:15. She put on her tank top, Speedo shorts and Reebok jogging shoes, the gold Seiko watch she used to time herself, and the gold chain and cross she always wore when jogging— her good luck charm, she liked to think. She then stepped out into the crisp morning air, did her stretching excercises there in the apartment courtyard, and headed out into the grayish morning light.

As Holly exited the apartment complex and onto Imperial Avenue, Douglas Childers was driving around aimlessly wondering how to get the drug money he needed to get back in the good graces of Luisa, his on- again, off-again girlfriend. It had been a rough night for Childers. Luisa had thrown him out of her house during an argument over drugs. The two had spent the better part of the night smoking crack cocaine and eating potato chips on the filthy couch in front of the TV set. When the coke ran out, so did Luisa's hospitality. In the heat of the argument that ensued, Childers threw Luisa against the living room wall. Luisa ran into the kitchen and returned with a greasy butcher knife, and screaming epithets in Spanish, chased Childers out into the yard. As he ran toward his battered pick-up truck in the driveway, Luisa threw the knife, which missed its mark and bounced off the hood of the truck.

In a rage, Childers picked up the knife and turned toward Luisa. Before he could reach her, however, she ran back inside the house and locked the door. He was tempted to kick it down, but he knew that Luisa kept a gun in the bedroom. In her present state of mind, she wouldn't hesitate to use it on him. He was right. As he turned to leave, Luisa flung the door open and fired two shots in his direction. He jumped into the cab of the truck and sped away.

He hadn't been gone long before he regretted his decision. It was a typically cool San Diego morning, and all he was wearing was a T-shirt and jeans. The heater in the battered Chevy pick-up had gone out years ago. He couldn't just go back and kiss and make up with Luisa. She was too mad right now. A few rocks of crack would do it, though.

He cruised around for the next 10 minutes trying to figure how to get money for the coke. He saw a convenience store ahead and figured it would be an easy hit. But as he approached the store, he saw a police car parked in front. "Shit," he screamed as he pounded the steering wheel in frustration. Cops were always screwing up his life. In fact, a cop had busted three of his ribs during an arrest four years ago. That arrest, for armed robbery, had sent Childers to the penitentiary for the second time.

The anger inside him rose as he began to wonder if he'd be able to get the necessary cash to score some coke. He started getting nervous as the early morning hits wore off. He made several turns and ended up lost, confused and raging mad on Imperial Avenue. Then he saw Holly Leyendecker.

Holly glanced at her gold Seiko watch as she ran. She had covered the first mile in approximately 10 minutes. Too slow. She needed to pick up her pace slightly. It felt good running in the morning. There was very little traffic to contend with, a good thing, since Holly, like many other joggers, seemed to go into a trance-like state as she ran. However, she did notice an old beat-up pick-up truck that passed her slowly.

"Hope you get your eyes full, creep," Holly thought to herself as the driver ogled her. But Douglas Childers wasn't just looking at her fabulous body, although he did like what he saw. Childers was more interested in the jewelry she might be wearing. As he slowly drove past, he thought he could see a gold chain around her neck and a watch on her wrist. They might be worth something, he thought. It was worth a shot, since it seemed to be the only option he had at the moment. Besides, it should be easy.

Six blocks up the street, Childers made a U-turn and pulled up to the curb on the opposite the side of the road from Holly. There was almost no traffic out yet, and this part of Imperial Avenue wasn't very well lighted. This might be a good place to

make his move. He could see Holly jogging up Imperial toward
his truck. He looked around, and seeing that there were no other
cars coming, slowly started driving in her direction.

Holly hadn't seen Childers' truck make the U-turn. She didn't
notice the truck until it was about a block up the street. Something clicked in her head that it might be the same truck that had
passed her a few moments ago, but she thought the driver was
just coming back to get another look at her. She glanced at her
watch, thinking this might be a good time to turn around and
head back toward her apartment. Suddenly, though, the truck
sped up and swerved over to her side of the street. In what
seemed like less than a second, Childers was out of the truck with
a knife aimed right at her throat.

Holly was too startled and too out of breath to scream. All she
could do was gasp, "Oh...God...no," between breaths as she
pedaled backward away from the knife. Childers grabbed her arm
roughly as she tried to break and run. "Gimme your watch or I'll
cut you to pieces," Childers said as he spun her around and flung
her toward the truck.

Thinking he was trying to force her inside, Holly brought her
left leg up against the truck and pushed back. In the panic of her
struggle, she thrust her elbow back forcefully, catching Childers
flush on the chin.

Childers screamed in rage. The anger poured out of him. He
brought the knife down with a thunderous blow that struck Holly
between the shoulder blades. Holly let out a horrified scream and
spun around in pain, snapping off the knife blade as she turned.
She tried to run, but made it only a few feet before she staggered
and collapsed in front of the truck.

Childers jumped into the truck, gunned the engine and
popped the clutch. It felt a little like running over a speed bump
as the left wheels of the truck bounced over Holly's body.

Childers peeled across Imperial Avenue and sped off. He glanced back in the mirror at Holly's mangled body lying beside the road. He felt no remorse for Holly—only disappointment that he had come up empty handed. He'd just have to look for another opportunity somewhere else.

Survival Analysis

The jogging craze has been a boon to shoe manufacturers, sporting goods stores—and muggers. The roadways, sidewalks and jogging trails are literally teeming with people of all ages getting in their daily exercise. Along the way, they have to dodge cars, bikes and barking dogs. They're usually so preoccupied with these things that they don't give much thought to being mugged, or even worse. But as illustrated by the Holly Leyendecker case, it's happening to joggers with greater frequency.

Like a lot of people, Holly did her running in the cool of the early morning hours. Not only was it cooler, she thought, but it was also safer. The only people up at this hour were other joggers and honest people on their way to work. Muggers didn't get up early in the morning. Douglas Childers proved her dead wrong.

Had Holly been more aware of the potential dangers, she would never have jogged alone. She became an instant target by virtue of the fact that she was a woman and she was alone. With a companion or two running with her, she probably would not have been singled out by Childers. It's very unusual for a mugger or rapist to attack someone in a group.

Even after Holly's suspicion was aroused by seeing the pick-up truck heading back toward her, she did not react with the degree of caution it takes to survive the age of crime. The very least Holly should have done was to keep a close eye on the truck. Any suspicion, no matter how slight, should be acted upon. By closely observing the truck, Holly might have been ready to react when the truck swerved across the road in her direction. She probably would have been able to evade Childers when he jumped out of the truck.

Here again, if Holly had been carrying a purse-size canister of chemical protection in the palm of her hand, she might have had time to fire at Childers before he grabbed her. Whether jogging, going to work or to the mall, a person alone should always carry a defensive chemical spray when venturing out of the house. This is particularly true of women.

Once the knife was at her throat, Holly had lost most of her options. In her case, trying to resist proved fatal. When an armed assailant is in your face, fighting back usually is not the best thing to do. The trick is to avoid letting an attacker get close enough to grab you. That requires both concentration and caution. In the long run, those are the best defenses against any type of crime.

How to Keep It from Happening to You

1. Never assume it can't happen to you.

2. Try to plan activities such as jogging during the daylight hours as much as possible. Darkness is the favorite cover of criminals.

3. Don't go it alone. Remember, there is a measure of safety in numbers.

4. Follow your instincts. If something arouses suspicion, be extremely cautious and try to take evasive action.

5. If you think someone is following you in a car, turn and go in the opposite direction. If your suspicions are confirmed, immediately try to get to a safe place and call for help.

6. Know the location of safe places along your route. If there are no safe places, find a safer jogging route within reach of a safe place (stores, service stations, fire stations, police stations).

7. Don't take jogging paths through dense woods or secluded areas unless you have several companions with you. Even then, exercise caution and watch out for suspicious-looking people.

8. Know the people out jogging with you. Some muggers and rapists go so far as to dress in jogging or other exercise attire to blend in and look less suspicious.

9. Carry a canister of The Protector chemical spray with you. It's available in a purse-size model you can clip onto your jogging shorts or carry in the palm of your hand.

6:15 a.m., Miami, Florida

Rosie Suarez dreaded the month of April when she had to set the clock ahead one hour for daylight savings time. That hour was literally as different as night and day for her. Instead of walking to the bus line in the light, she'd have to walk it in the darkness for the next six months.

Until a couple of years ago, Rosie had felt perfectly at ease making the six-block walk to the bus stop. At 61, she wasn't as agile as she used to be, and the city had let the sidewalks deteriorate to the point it was like running an obstacle course. Also, the neighborhood had gradually changed, and she didn't feel nearly as safe as she once did. It had always been a poor neighborhood, but most of the people who lived there were honest and hard working. But lately, there had been sporadic drug dealing in the area, and it had spread into the neighborhood. The last couple of months or so, she began noticing the presence of strangers in the neighborhood. Still, she felt relatively safe making the walk during the months when it was light outside at 6:30 a.m. Walking it in the darkness was a different story. She felt very uneasy about it.

But she had no choice. Life had to go on. The bus was the only only way she could get to her housekeeping job at a Miami hotel across town. She had held the job for more than 20 years, and if she could just hang on four more years, she'd be able to retire. Her retirement was very important to her, since she was a widow with no family to help her in her old age.

Her husband had died of tuberculosis shortly after they arrived in Miami from Mexico more than 25 years ago. She and her husband had desperately wanted children, but she was never able to get pregnant. Rosie would watch in envy as her neighbors with all their kids got together for loud, boisterous holiday celebrations. Occasionally, she was invited over, but for the most part, her life was lonely and uneventful. Of course, now, most of her old neighbors had moved on to better things, and the element that had replaced them made Rosie uncomfortable to the point of becoming reclusive. These days, her only contact with the outside world was her job at the hotel and grocery shopping at a store near her bus stop.

Just as she had done every morning for the past 20 years, Rosie put on her crisp maid's uniform and went out the door at precisely 6:30 a.m. to walk the six blocks to catch the 6:55 bus. The walk only took 10 minutes, but Rosie had a dread fear of missing her bus, thinking that she would lose her job if she were late to work. As always, she cradled the handle of her purse in the crook of her elbow as she carefully made her way along the cracked and broken sidewalk toward the bus stop.

Humidity already hung heavy in the morning air. It was going to be another steamy day in Miami. But Rosie Suarez wouldn't have to suffer through it. She would die suddenly and swiftly.

It seemed darker than usual to Rosie this morning. The nearest street light was two blocks up the street, and Rosie was having a difficult time maneuvering around the cracks and bulges in the uneven pavement. As she approached the street light, she could see a little better and was able to quicken her pace. She walked under the street light and back into the darkness where she had to slow down again.

Gerald Williams was sitting on the curb a block up the street when he spotted Rosie as she passed under the street light. Gerald was an 18-year-old with a gnawing hunger for crack cocaine. He had spent the night doing crack at a house in the neighborhood, but when his money ran out, so did his welcome. Rosie was his ticket back inside the house.

Rosie never actually saw Gerald. After coming out of the light, her eyes hadn't fully adjusted to the darkness. All she heard was his desperate command.

"Give me the purse!"

"Wha...," Rosie tried to respond in her confusion. She didn't even finish the word.

"Give me the purse, now!" Gerald demanded angrily through clinched teeth as he grabbed the purse. Rosie instinctively brought her hands together in a cowering motion. In an attempt to dislodge the purse from the crook of her elbow, Gerald swung around to his right, propelling Rosie like a kid at the end of a pop-the-whip line, face first into large tree.

The sound of her head hitting the tree left no doubt that her skull was crushed. Had anyone been on the street within earshot that morning, they would have recognized the sound of human flesh and bone being smashed with great force into an immovable object.

Rosie didn't scream or yell. It happened so quickly there simply was no time. The only sound she made was a slight whimper as the life left her body.

"I told you to give me the purse, didn't I, huh, didn't I?" Gerald screamed as he savagely kicked her lifeless body. Then he reached down, grabbed the purse off her arm and casually walked away with Rosie's purse and the $12.34 it contained.

An hour later, a passerby found her body and called the police. Her death might have gone unsolved were it not for Gerald's need for crack cocaine. The next night, he was shot and killed while trying to rob a liquor store. Evidence found on his body implicated him in Rosie's death, and her case was closed without further investigation.

Survival Analysis

In a very real sense, Rosie Suarez never knew what hit her. It all happened so quickly with her assailant coming at her out of the darkness, Rosie didn't even see his face.

Perhaps the biggest mistake she made was walking alone in the darkness without a flashlight. With a light to aid her, she might have been able to see far enough up the street to have spotted Gerald. Darkness is one of the best allies of criminals.

A flashlight also would have made it safer for Rosie to walk in the street instead of on the cracked and broken sidewalk. It was a side street without much auto traffic, and she would have been somewhat less vulnerable in that she might have been able to see her attacker coming at her.

But what then? Even if she had seen Gerald, there wasn't much she could do to defend herself. This is another case for carrying a high-quality chemical protection spray. We recommend that everyone, especially women, carry a military grade chemical spray that will incapacitate a mugger for up to 30 minutes. Rosie Suarez might be alive today if she had had a purse-size canister of the chemical with her that morning.

That is not to say Rosie should have confronted her assailant. All too often, self-defense weapons—especially guns—give citizens a false sense of security. If Rosie had seen Gerald and felt threatened, her best course of action would have been to turn around and walk back home, keeping an eye over her shoulder as she did so. Once back inside her home (with the doors locked), she could have called the police. Even if it meant being late for work, it would have been far better than being killed.

She also could have screamed for help. A woman screaming at that time of the morning might have alerted neighbors. If she had screamed "Fire!", it almost assuredly would have attracted attention.

But even without having a flashlight or tear gas, or being unable to scream for help, Rosie Suarez might have lived to tell about it had she been carrying her purse differently. Gerald didn't set out to kill Rosie. What he wanted most was her purse. Carrying it as she did in the crook of her elbow made it difficult for her to comply with Gerald's demand, especially when she drew her arms up to her body. Rosie's best bet would have been to carry the purse in her hand and to have dropped it instantly upon Gerald's command. Elderly women are often injured when purse snatchers grab a purse off the shoulder or arm. In Rosie's case, the injuries were fatal.

How to Keep It from Happening to You

1. Never lose sight of the fact that you are vulnerable to crime every time you walk out the door of your home.

2. Try to avoid walking alone down dark, lonely streets.

3. Always carry a flashlight with you at night. Not only will it help you see better, it can also be used as a defense weapon if you are attacked.

4. If you feel threatened, immediately turn around and walk in the opposite direction.

5. Don't be timid about screaming for help if you feel threatened. Screaming "fire" usually gets the most attention.

6. If you know you are being pursued by a potential assailant, do whatever is necessary to attract attention—even if it means running up to a house and breaking a window to alert the people inside.

7. Stay as far away as possible from shrubs, trees, parked cars and buildings where muggers can lay in wait. In many cases, it's actually safer to walk in the middle of the street.

8. Don't carry your purse over your shoulder or in the crook of your elbow. Hold it in your hand so there's less likelihood of being injured if someone tries to snatch it. Better yet, carry your purse upside down, with your hand on the latch. If a mugger demands your purse, open the latch and spill the contents on the ground. This will force the mugger to rummage around on the ground to find valuables, giving you time to get away from the scene.

9. If a mugger demands your purse or wallet, do not resist. It's better to lose money and other valuables than to risk being killed or injured in a fight with a desperate person. Once you comply with the mugger's demands, leave the scene immediately. Return home or to a safe place to call the police.

10. DON'T CARRY A GUN UNLESS YOU'RE ABSO-LUTELY CERTAIN YOU COULD USE IT. There's always the chance it could be taken away and used against you. Remember, too, a gun won't do you much good if you can't get it out of your purse or pocket in time. In many cases, you would have to walk around with the gun in your hand in order to have time to use it. Not only would that be very dangerous, it also might get you arrested. Instead of a gun, we recommend a powerful, reliable chemical spray that you can hold in your hand, ready to ward off potential assailants in an instant.

9:15 a.m., Dallas, Texas

C arlos didn't plan to commit murder. All Carlos planned to do was get in the house, take what he wanted and get out as fast as he could. Carlos was a small-time burglar whose entire existence involved getting money, getting drugs, getting high and, if he was lucky, not getting busted. He had already done two stints in the penitentiary and was careful not to repeat the same mistakes that had led to previous arrests and convictions.

Had circumstances in his life been different, Carlos might have been a successful politician, for he had mastered the art of subterfuge and deceit. Posing as a lawn care man, Carlos was able to cruise affluent north Dallas neighborhoods without arousing any suspicion whatsoever. He even went so far as to haul a small flat-bed trailer, complete with lawn mower and gardening tools, behind his van. When he backed into the driveway of the target house, it looked perfectly normal. He always brought along a sidekick who'd pretend to work in the yard while serving as a lookout.

Carlos had little to worry about at Jim and Pam Martinson's house on a quiet street of well-kept homes in a fashionable neighborhood. The house was well shielded from view with lush shrubbery and landscaping which afforded the Martinson's the privacy they sought. Carlos had been watching the house for several days and knew that no one was home at 9:00 in the morning on a workday. Had he been a day earlier, he would have been right.

At 7:45 that morning, Jim Martinson kissed his wife good-bye and left for his office in downtown Dallas. Pam normally would have left at the same time for her job at the Dallas Market Center. But on this particular Friday, Pam had taken the day off to catch up on some work around the house. Also, the BMW was scheduled for service today and she wouldn't have transportation.

When the doorbell rang at 8:00, Pam opened the front door without even checking to see who was there. She was expecting the driver from the dealership to pick up the car. Owning a BMW does has its privileges. Pam signed the work order, gave the driver the keys and returned to the breakfast table to finish the morning paper. The day was so pretty, Pam decided to take her coffee and newspaper out on the patio. In fact, the weather was so nice on this April day that Pam left the sliding glass door open when she went back inside to take a shower nearly an hour later. But that was nothing particularly out of the ordinary. They rarely kept the back doors locked when someone was home. After all, this was a very safe neighborhood. In fact, in the 15 years the Martinsons had lived here, they knew of only one burglary, and that had been several years ago. Sure, they had an alarm system, but it had never once been used. The Martinsons simply never thought about crime. That was something that only happened in other neighborhoods, certainly not theirs.

Pam slipped out of her robe and looked at her body in the mirror of the master bath. At 55, and with two college-age kids, she was still attractive. Yet she wasn't satisfied with her image in the mirror. She vowed once again to lay off the sweets and get back on her exercise program. She sucked in her stomach, sighed and stepped into the shower.

They say that timing is everything. In this case it was. Just as Pam was finishing her shower, Carlos was coming through the back gate. Even a seasoned burglar like Carlos was amazed. The yard had a nice brick fence for complete privacy. And would you look at that! The sliding glass door was wide open.

"Man, they put out the welcome mat for me," Carlos thought to himself. "Who could refuse an invitation like this?" Carlos stepped inside and grinned with pleasure as he looked around at all the treasure. VCR, stereo, TV, computer. He would get those last. He headed up the stairs to the master bedroom where most people keep their jewelry and cash. It was to his right at the head of the stairs. He headed straight for the jewelry box on the dressing table across the room, quickly grabbing the contents and stuffing them into the plastic garbage bag he carried. Then he pulled out the top drawer and emptied the contents on the floor.

Pam heard the noise and stopped toweling her hair to listen. Thinking the cat had knocked over something, she angrily flung open the bathroom door, expecting to find the cat on her furniture. She found Carlos instead. Like electricity, numbness and confusion swept through her body. Instinctively, she pulled the towel up to cover her naked body and gave a startled yelp.

Carlos saw her in the mirror above the dressing table and whirled to face her. "Just cool it lady, and nobody gets hurt," Carlos said softly as he stepped toward her.

Now in a panic, Pam screamed, "What do you want? Get out, get out! I'll call the police," she yelled as she reached for the phone by the bed.

Carlos lunged across the room, grabbed the phone out of her hand and knocked her back on the bed with his body on top of her. Pam's panic turned to hysteria. She began flailing wildly with her one free hand, sobbing and screaming at the top of her lungs. As Carlos tried to cover her mouth to stifle her screams, she bit down on his hand as hard as she could. That sent Carlos into a fit of rage. His first punch glanced off her forehead, causing her to scream in pain. The next three punches landed squarely on her nose and cheek. It wasn't until the fifth or sixth punch that Pam lay silent on the bed. However, even that didn't stop the assault on her body. Something in Carlos had snapped. He continued to beat her until his hands began to ache. Then he picked up a brass lamp and used it like a baseball bat on her head and face. He continued to beat her long after she was dead.

Carlos' fingerprints were found on the lamp. He was identified and charged with murder. Three days later, he was arrested in South Texas, trying to make his way to Mexico. The day before Carlos' capture, Pam Martinson had been buried. Her face was so disfigured from the beating the casket was kept closed during the ceremony.

Survival Analysis

What makes Pam Martinson's death so tragic is the fact that it could have easily been prevented. Pam did not have to die from that chance encounter with a burglar in her bedroom. Had she followed a few simple procedures for survival in this age of crime, she would almost surely be alive today.

Pam violated the most basic rule of survival. She made herself an easy target. To begin with, the outside of the Martinson home was shielded from the view of neighbors who might have found the situation suspicious—had they been able to see the strange van parked in the driveway. The high shrubs and trees in the front and the brick fence in back provided plenty of cover for Carlos to do his dirty work. Also, had there been a Neighborhood Watch program in effect, one of the neighbors might have been on the lookout for anything evenly remotely suspicious going on at their house. Most Neighborhood Watch programs are clearly marked with road signs to help discourage would-be burglars, which offers the distinct possibility that Carlos would have avoided their neighborhood altogether.

In actuality, Pam was extremely vulnerable to crime long before Carlos came along. The Martinsons (and their neighbors) had been lulled into a false sense of security by their "safe" neighborhood. The fact that there hadn't been a burglary there in years created the illusion that there was nothing to worry about. A burglary simply couldn't happen in their neighborhood.

Perhaps that's why Pam answered the front door when it rang earlier that morning. Had the person at the door been, say, a rapist instead of the driver from the BMW dealership, Pam might have already been dead when Carlos came calling. It's foolhardy for anyone in any neighborhood to open the door without knowing for sure who's there. Had Pam been alert to the possibility of danger, she would have looked through the peephole to identify the person at the door. Then, talking through the closed door, she would have asked the person to provide some kind of identification to prove he was who he said he was. That may seem excessive, but people who take extreme measures to protect themselves against crime are usually the ones who live to tell about it.

Pam also could have been attacked sitting alone on the back patio. Remember, the gate was unlocked, and there's a high fence around the backyard. Of course, her worst lapse in caution was leaving the back door open when she went back inside. It was indeed an open invitation, and Carlos gladly accepted.

However, even after Carlos was in the house, even when she was face-to-face with him, Pam still had several opportunities to save her life. When Pam first heard the noise, she was still in the bathroom. Rather than barging out expecting to find a cat, she should have anticipated the worst: an intruder in her home. The most prudent thing to do would be remain in the bathroom with the door locked. Had the Mortinsons prepared for the possibilities of crime in advance, they might have converted their bathroom into a "safe haven" inside the home. In that case, the bathroom would have had a solid core door with deadbolt. It would have been equipped with an extension phone and possibly a panic button linked to the home security system. They might even have kept some type of self-defense weapon in the bathroom cabinet, such as a high-quality chemical spray.

Even though the Mortinson's bathroom wasn't so equipped, it still offered greater safety than being in the bedroom with a burglar. By returning to the bathroom and locking the door behind her, she might have been able to open the window and scream for help. Putting any kind of barrier between yourself and an intruder is better than an open confrontation. Remember, Carlos was all the way across the room when she first saw him. Her retreat to the bathroom would have given Carlos a clear avenue of escape, and he might have taken it. Confronting Carlos was the worst thing Pam could have done.

But there still was time to get to the bathroom even after Carlos turned on her. Reaching for the phone and threatening to call the police as Carlos was advancing on her clearly wasn't a wise move on Pam's part. Of course, she was in a panic and unable to think clearly. The fact that she was naked probably heightened her panic by making her feel more vulnerable.

How to Keep It from Happening to You

1. Don't ever think crime can't happen to you. Nothing makes you more vulnerable than a false sense of security.

2. If you suspect a burglar in your home, don't go to investigate. If at all possible, shut and lock a door between you and the burglar. Then call the police, or open a window and scream for help. Your best option is to get out of the house altogether if you can do so without endangering your life. Once you're out of the house, run to a neighbor's and call the police.

3. Don't confront the burglar. Chances are, if you don't provoke him, he won't harm you. Most burglars just want to get out of the house once they've been detected. Let them go! The worst thing you can do is try to prevent the burglar's escape.

4. Create a "safe haven" inside your home where you can retreat in the event of an attack. Ideally, this should be a room that offers an avenue of escape, like a bathroom or bedroom with a window. The room should have a solid-core door with at least a 1" deadbolt you can latch from inside. Have an exten-

sion phone inside the room along with emergency phone numbers. If you have an alarm system, install a panic button so you can sound an alarm from inside the room.

5. If you come face-to-face with a burglar, try to stay as calm and in control of your actions as possible. That will enable you to think more clearly and possibly find a safe way out of the situation. Also, the calmer you are, the less threatening you appear to the burglar. Remember, the burglar probably wants to get out of the house as badly as you want him out.

6. Don't fight the intruder unless you are attacked. In that case, fight back with anything at your disposal. However, don't pull a gun unless you're sure you can use it. Otherwise, the burglar might end up using it on you. One alternative to a gun is a high-quality chemical spray that incapacitates the intruder without causing permanent physical damage. Some brands, such as The Protector, are effective from as far away as 15 feet. Keep a canister on a bedside table as well as in your "safe haven".

7. Develop an escape plan for every room in your home, and rehearse it regularly. If you have an alarm system with panic buttons, always keep their location fresh in your mind (it's easy to forget where things like these are located when you seldom use them).

8. If you return home and see evidence your home has been burglarized, get out of the house at once. The thief may still be inside. Go to a neighbor's house and call the police, then wait for the police to arrive. Don't try to enter the house and apprehend the thief yourself!

9. Never leave doors or windows unlocked, even when you're home. And always know who's at the door before you open

it. Look out the window or use a peephole to identify the person at the door.

10. Make your home as visible as possible from the street. Tall shrubs and high fences give burglars plenty of cover to move about without being seen by neighbors or passing motorists. Use floodlighting and porch lighting to keep your home visible during the evening hours. And always try to create the illusion that someone is at home at all times. Most burglars will not enter a house if they think someone is inside.

10:30 a.m., New Orleans, Louisiana

Dunbrook Forest was a quiet neighborhood 13 miles northeast of downtown New Orleans in Slidell. The families who lived there were active in the children's PTO school meetings, community swimming meets, sponsored tennis leagues and golf tournaments. On the Fourth of July, block parties were arranged, months in advance, and collectively they shot off fireworks to celebrate the nation's birthday. Christmas was a time of lights and animated cut-outs with one of Santa's helpers on every corner. Dunbrook Forest was one of those rare places in America where families lived and played as a family.

One of those families, the Braxton's, lived in a two-story four-bedroom home on a cul-de-sac in the front of the community. Jeff and Carrie Braxton, both 41 years old, had moved there shortly after their first child was born. Jeff worked for an oil exploration company, and Carrie worked in the home as chauffeur, cook, housekeeper, nurse and seamstress. Both were deliriously happy with their lives—until one fateful morning. On that day, Carrie's world fell off its axis and the sun began rising in the west.

Cecil Hardman was quite familiar with Dunbrook Forest. He did the lawn maintenance for a number of home owners, including the Braxtons. He carried his mower, edger, broom and blower in the back of his 1971 pick-up. The truck was a rolling disaster spewing blue smoke and backfiring every time it was started. Nonetheless, it got Cecil from one lawn to the next each and every week.

Most of his customers agreed that Cecil was one of the hardest workers they had ever seen. He would cut, edge and sweep a yard expertly and inexpensively. He took great care that the yard was fertilized at the appropriate times and watered frequently to ensure healthy growth. Cecil Hardman thought of himself more as a gardener than a lawn man. His pride in his work showed throughout the neighborhood.

Today, Cecil was scheduled to do the Braxton's yard. He normally arrived about 7:45 in the morning and was finished by 10 o'clock or so. When he hadn't shown up by 9:30, Carrie decided she ought to call and see if he was all right. She knew Cecil was having problems with his truck, and taking into consideration its overall condition, a breakdown on the freeway would not only be understandable, but very likely. Her concern was not completely unselfish, however. Carrie had planned a surprise birthday party for her best friend and tennis doubles partner, Susan, that afternoon and wanted the yard absolutely perfect when the guests arrived. There was no answer at his home when she called.

Carrie heard Lucky, their cocker spaniel, whimpering and remembered it was time for his walk. "Hang on buddy, I'll be right back," she said to Lucky as she went upstairs to change clothes. Standing in front of her full length mirror, she smiled at her reflection.

After 19 years of marriage and three kids, she still had a pretty nice figure. Her 109 pounds were evenly distributed over her five foot three frame. She applied fresh lipstick and brushed her short blond hair. Carrie never left the house without her make-up being perfect and every hair in place.

She put the leash on Lucky and picked up her keys. She smiled at the small can of MACE attached to the key ring. Jeff had bought it on impulse at the sporting goods store and insisted she take it with her every time she left the house. That had been over a year ago, and she hadn't been in a situation where she even considered using the stuff. Dunbrook Forest was considered by most of its residents to be a safe place to walk, day or night, because the Civic Association had hired a security company to circulate a marked vehicle through the neighborhood 24 hours a day. Jeff Braxton had fought the idea of a security company, preferring an off-duty police officer instead. But he had lost the argument. Not that it mattered really. There had been virtually no crime in the subdivision for more than a year, and that had been the work of several neighborhood teen-agers. Certainly nothing to get overly alarmed about.

Carrie felt very much at ease as she started down the block with Lucky. If only Cecil Hardman had shown up to do the yard, she wouldn't have a worry in the world. In a matter of minutes, all that would change.

Carrie and Lucky had walked about five blocks when a black mini-van drove by. As it passed them, it slowed down slightly in what Carrie thought was a precaution since she was walking in the street. That was the one thing that rankled Carrie about

Dunbrook Forest. Why on earth didn't the developer put in sidewalks? Carrie had never seen the van in the neighborhood, but then, it was a fairly large area and she couldn't possibly recognize every vehicle. The van turned off at the stop sign a block down the street.

A minute or two later, the mini-van came by again, this time from the opposite direction. Although the windows were darkly tinted, she could see the driver, a rough looking character with stringy black hair. The van slowed down again as it passed her, and she could tell the driver was giving her the once over. In a way, it pleased her that she could still elicit such looks from a stranger. In another way, it frightened her. This guy surely wasn't from around here. Now, she was glad she had the MACE with her just in case.

Her first impulse was to turn around, go back home and call the security company. But then she decided to complete her walk. After all, nothing really bad ever happened in Dunbrook Forest. The driver was probably just a repairman looking for the right address. She was relieved when she looked back and saw the van was gone. Just to be on the safe side, she took the can of MACE from her pocket and kept it in the palm of her right hand.

Carrie's normal routine was to walk a couple of blocks further, turn down a side street, then walk back up the next street over. As she rounded the corner, she saw the black mini-van parked on the side-street. She hesitated slightly, but not seeing anyone in the van, kept walking toward it. Suddenly, just as she was alongside the van, the long-haired driver popped out from behind the van and lunged at her. Carrie screamed and Lucky started barking furiously as the man grabbed the left hand holding the leash and started pulling her toward the side door of the van. Carrie instinctively fired the MACE she was holding in her right hand. The man grimaced and wiped at his face with his free hand, trying to wipe the MACE out of his eyes, cursing her furiously all the while. In spite of the shot of MACE, he still held Carrie's left arm firmly, and she lost her grip on the leash. Snarling, Lucky grabbed the man's pants leg and began tugging at it wildly.

The man quickly shrugged off the effects of the MACE, kicked Lucky three feet into the air and landed a hard blow to Carrie's mid-section. She dropped the canister of MACE as she doubled over in pain. The man threw Carrie into the van, jumped in behind her and slammed the side door shut. Then he forced her onto her back and quickly tied her hands as she continued to sob and scream. To silence her, he ripped off a piece of duct tape and placed it over her mouth. As Carrie sobbed and gasped for breath through her nose, the man climbed over the bench seat, started the van and sped off.

At that very moment, Cecil Hardman was arriving at the Braxton house. He rang the doorbell several times. Not getting an answer, Cecil walked around to the back of the house. The Braxton's next door neighbor, who had gone out to put a letter in the mailbox, noticed Cecil's truck in the driveway. She would report this fact to the police in less than four hours.

Ten minutes later, the black mini-van crossed under I-10 heading south. The driver glanced back and saw that the woman was still tightly bound. "Damn, I got me a good one here," the driver said to Carrie. "Darlin', we're gonna have ourselves some fun. Yessiree, lots of fun," he giggled as he turned his attention back to the road ahead. Within 15 minutes, he reached the dirt road turn-off that would take him and his "toy" to the mobile home centered in the middle of nine acres of dense, swampy forest. There she could scream her fool head off and nobody would hear, or, for that matter, pay much attention if they did.

He pulled up in front of the mobile home and honked the horn twice. Several men holding beer cans came out. Carrie Braxton gasped in horror when the van's side door slid open. She saw not one, but four men staring at her.

"Look what I brought home for desert," the driver laughed as he stood by the open door. "It was as easy as pluckin' a pear from a tree."

Buster, the biggest of the three men, reached into the van and gave Carrie Braxton a big, yellow-toothed smile. "Pleased to make your acquaintance, mam," Buster said sarcastically. Then in one sweeping motion, he snatched the duct tape from her mouth, nearly ripping her lips off with it. "Why, looky here," Buster said, "she ain't got nothin' to say...not even a friendly howdy do." The others joined Buster in laughter. They continued to laugh as tears rolled down Carrie's cheeks. Then to Carrie, "Guess you were in the wrong place at the wrong time."

"She sprayed something in my face that burned like hell," the driver said to Buster. "She's lucky to still be alive...I nearly killed her then and there."

"Now, what would you want to go and do a thing like that for?" Buster asked jokingly. "This is a fine lookin' lady. Yessiree, mighty fine. She wouldn't be much fun dead, now would she?" Grabbing Carrie by the shoulders, Buster pulled her up and out of the van.

As a little girl, Carrie had been afraid of the dark. She had imagined all kinds of monsters lurking in the dark. Darkness meant evil. For the next two hours, Carrie sat bound and gagged inside a small, pitch-dark closet. The difference between her adult and childhood fear of the dark was that the monsters in this place existed in the light. The light outside of the closet.

When the door finally opened, Buster pulled her roughly out of the closet and guided her down a narrow hall into the squalid living area of the mobile home. Everything was a blur to Carrie. She thought there were five men and several women. They were all dressed in a similar fashion: dark shirts, jeans and heavy boots. The thought ran through Carrie's mind that the group was some kind of cult. Carrie would never know.

By approximately 2:15 a.m., Carrie had been raped twelve times. Her naked body showed signs of numerous beatings and cigarette burns. She had been unconscious for at least an hour. Her captors, possibly thinking she was dead, had dumped her in a rural area north of Interstate 10. When she regained consciousness, she had somehow made her way to the side of a road where she was found by a passing motorist at 5:20 a.m.

A few hours later, Cecil Hardman was released from jail. He had been arrested as a suspect in the disappearance of Carrie Braxton. Although exonerated, Cecil never cut another lawn in Dunbrook Forest.

Two weeks after Carrie was released from the hospital, the Braxtons put their home up for sale and moved to Des Moine, Iowa, where they now live.

Carrie's kidnappers were never caught.

Survival Analysis

Carrie Braxton's case is important for a number of reasons. First, it points up the growing arrogance of criminals. They know that law enforcement officials are stretched way beyond the breaking point and that even in broad daylight a criminal has a better than average chance of getting away with a crime. Secondly, it illustrates the importance of being on guard all the time, even in the safest neighborhoods. Thirdly, it demonstrates the fallibility of some self-defense materials.

A few years ago, it would have been unheard of for someone to attempt to abduct an adult from a neighborhood like Dunbrook Forest, especially in broad daylight! The drug culture has had a lot to do with changing the pattern of crime in this country. Many of today's criminals are drug addicts who have totally lost touch with reality. They will do anything to anybody anytime the opportunity presents itself.

Carrie Braxton had the misfortune of being that opportunity. She was simply in the wrong place at the wrong time. Had she left her house a few minutes later, she would never have encountered the black van and its driver. Surprisingly, Carrie continued up the street after the van had driven by the second time, slowing down to check her out both times. That was her biggest mistake. The driver was definitely exhibiting suspicious behavior. At that point, Carrie should have followed her first inclination to return home and call the neighborhood security patrol. While she was at it, she also should have called the police to report the incident. Had she been able to give the police the license number and a description of the van, they could have run a check on its owner.

Carrie clearly felt some degree of concern, because she took the can of MACE from her pocket and had it at the ready. Had

Carrie taken the time to read the disclaimers on the can, she
would have known that MACE has little effect on someone who
is on drugs. In light of the driver's aggressive behavior, there was
good reason to suspect he might be under the influence of drugs.

Even if she had been carrying a military-grade chemical
protection like The Protector (a product powerful enough to
incapacitate even an assailant on drugs), it still would not be
prudent to run the risk of a confrontation. There is certainly no
disgrace in retreating to the safety of your home in a situation like
this. Had Carrie turned back, she would not have suffered the
horrible pain and indignation of her ordeal. The only time to fight
is when you have no other choice. The rest of the time, it is far
better to try and avoid such encounters altogether.

It's sad that we can't walk the streets of our neighborhoods in
broad daylight without some degree of fear for our safety. Unfortunately, that's the way it is in virtually every city in this country.

How to Keep It from Happening to You.

1. Just because you're walking in a "safe" neighborhood, don't
    drop your guard. Be cautious all the time. If you feel threat-
    ened, return home and call the police.

2. Avoid walking alone at night. If you live in a high-crime area,
    don't walk at night, period.

3. Avoid walking on dimly lit streets or through alleys and
    tunnels. Never take shortcuts through lightly traveled areas.
    Stay in well- lighted areas as much as possible.

4. Walk on the part of the sidewalk closest to the street, as far
    away as possible from shrubs, trees and doorways. You may
    even be safer walking in the street than on the sidewalk.

5. Walk confidently, directly and at a steady pace. Walk on the side of the street facing oncoming traffic.

6. Be careful if someone stops you and asks for directions. Always reply from a safe distance. Never get too close to the car.

7. Wear shoes and clothing that give you freedom of movement. You might end up having to run for your life.

12:40 p.m., Los Angeles, California

Ellie Daniels was tempted to fall into bed and crash.
The flight from Amsterdam to Los Angeles had been
almost two hours late, and after nearly 14 hours of
walking up and down the aisle of a 747, she was exhausted. She
had just checked into the Hotel Marquis where her airline flight
crew stayed during layovers in Los Angeles. As tempting as the
bed looked, however, Ellie forced herself to unpack her bag and
take a shower.

Ellie hated staying at the Hotel Marquis. It was large, cold
and impersonal, a far cry from the Wilshire where flight crews
used to stay in better times. Her airline had been flying under the
protection of Chapter 11 bankruptcy for more than a year, and
when the the company started retrenching, hotel accommodations
for flight crews had been downgraded considerably. What she
disliked most was having to stay on the 11th floor. She always
felt uncomfortable on the upper floors of hotels, which struck her

as odd for someone who spent most of her life at 20,000 feet. But she remembered seeing news footage of people trapped in high-rise hotel fires, and those terrible images had stuck with her.

Derek Coleman had no way of knowing Ellie Daniels worried about hotel fires. It was purely coincidental. Hotel smoke detectors were, in a way, important to his livelihood. Derek Coleman did much of his work in the Hotel Marquis, not as an employee, but as a thief and rapist. He also worked several other hotels in the Los Angeles area, but favored the Marquis because of its lax security. In the past eight months, he had burglarized 10 rooms, robbed four guests at gunpoint and raped three women. And still, he was able to come and go at will in the hotel.

In fact, Derek Coleman was more familiar with the Hotel Marquis than many of its employees. He knew where security cameras were positioned. He knew the best access to the hotel from the street (there were three entrances). And he knew that during the day, there was only one security guard on duty, along with a hotel detective. At night, the hotel beefed up security with four guards, still not nearly enough security for a 22-story hotel with 1,400 rooms.

Derek always did his dirty work during the day because it was so much easier. People tend to be a little more cautious at night. Few worried about anything happening during the day, especially in a hotel like the Marquis, and most certainly not inside the confines of their locked hotel room. But that's where Derek was in his element.

Derek's job was made easier by the fact that he had accumulated more than a dozen room keys during the time he had been working the Marquis. Posing as a maintenance worker on the hotel staff, Derek would enter hotel rooms, ostensibly to check out smoke alarms. Sometimes he would do it when a maid had the room open for cleaning. While the maid was cleaning the bathroom, he would quickly rifle the bedroom, scooping up anything of value, including the room key that might have been carelessly left by the guest. But Derek had learned that this technique rarely netted more than pocket change.

Several months ago, Derek had developed a scheme that netted him a lot more money, along with some very pleasant fringe benefits—as Ellie Daniels was about to discover.

Ellie had just finished drying her hair when Derek Coleman called. At the Marquis, he could dial the room direct from any number of house phones located throughout the hotel. He had called four rooms before he found one occupied by a woman.

"Hello, this is hotel maintenance," Derek said when Ellie picked up the phone. "We had a report this morning that the smoke detector wasn't activated. Would you check to see if the red light on the smoke alarm is showing?"

Ellie looked up at the smoke alarm and saw that the red light was on. "Yes, the light is on," Ellie said. "Who reported it as not working?" Ellie asked with slight concern.

"I'm not sure mam," Derek replied politely. "It was at 10:30 this morning."

"I just checked in a little while ago," Ellie replied. "It must have been someone who had the room before me. But it seems to be working fine."

"Could be a weak battery. If you'd like, we can come and check it out," Derek said.

"Well, yeah, I'd like to know it's working. Could you do it right away, though? I've been flying all night, and I'm about to get some sleep," Ellie said.

"We're sorry for the inconvenience. We'll send someone right up. It won't take but a minute," Derek replied.

A few minutes later, Derek Coleman knocked on the door and said, "Hotel maintenance." He was wearing gray work pants and a matching shirt. He had a tool belt slung over his shoulder.

He didn't need the disguise, however. Ellie opened the door without even checking the peep-hole. She was wearing only a terry cloth bath robe. Derek Coleman liked what he saw in the 29-year-old with jet-black hair and smooth olive complexion. He immediately knew he would take more than just her money.

"Sorry to bother you, mam," Derek said as he stepped into the room. The door swung shut behind him and automatically locked. "This won't take but a minute," he said as he stepped over beneath the smoke detector and laid his tool belt on the floor. He stooped down with his back to her and popped the snap on the belt's pouch. When he stood up and turned around, he was holding a gun. Before she knew what was happening, he grabbed her by the arm, pulled her to him and shoved the gun under her nose.

"Don't scream, don't make trouble and nobody gets hurt," he said softly.

"Okay, okay," Ellie said calmly trying to stay in control of the situation, "just take what you want and go. My purse is on the table." As part of her flight attendant training, Ellie had been well schooled in remaining calm in the face of emergencies.

"Yeah, I'll take the money. But first, I want some of this," Derek said as he pulled the cord on her bath robe.

All the training in the world couldn't have prepared Ellie for the feeling that swept over her. She was being violated—first her privacy, and now her body. Anger boiled up inside her, and she gritted her teeth and lashed out at Derek with her free hand. "Leave me alone! Get out of here," she screamed as she flailed at Derek and tried to pull away.

Derek responded with a vicious blow to Ellie's cheek with the butt of the gun handle. As Ellie screamed in pain, Derek pushed her back on the bed, and quickly put his hand over her mouth. He was right on top of her as he softly said, "I told you to be good and nobody would get hurt." He held up the gun and said, "If you want some more of this, you'll get it. What's it gonna be?" He carefully removed his hand from her mouth for her reply.

The pain of the blow had taken all the fight out of Ellie. She knew she had no other choice at this point but to comply. "I'll do whatever you want," she choked out a reply through her sobs. "Don't hurt me...I'll do what you want."

"Good girl," Derek said as he loosened the belt on his trousers. "Who knows, you might even enjoy this. I know I will," Derek said as he roughly pushed her legs apart.

Before leaving her room, Derek Coleman took Ellie's cash, credit cards and jewelry. He ripped the phone out of the wall and tied her up with the cord. He vowed he would track her down and kill her if she told anybody what had happened.

Thirty minutes after Derek left, Ellie staggered to a house phone down the hall and called the front desk. Several minutes later, the hotel detective rushed to the eleventh floor and found Ellie crying hysterically in the hallway. She was taken to the hospital and treated for broken bones in her cheek. A team of women from the Rape Crisis Center came to carefully gather evidence.

It took Ellie more than six weeks to recover from the injury to her face. She still has a slight indentation in her cheek as a permanent reminder of her ordeal. She has emotional scars that don't show, but that are even more pronounced.

Derek Coleman continued to work the Hotel Marquis for nearly a year before he was captured and convicted. He is currently serving a 25-year sentence in a California prison.

Ellie Daniels returned to work as a flight attendant. However, she now carries a portable smoke alarm, security alarm and door lock which she religiously uses at every hotel where she stays. She never opens the door when someone knocks.

Survival Analysis

"Hotel security" is an oxymoron in the truest sense. Moreover, it is almost impossible for hotels to provide adequate security for the protection of their guests. With thousands of total strangers checking in and out of a hotel each week, it is virtually impossible for a hotel's staff to tell who is a guest and who is an intruder. Hotel keys change hands daily. Many guests either neglect to turn in their keys—or keep them for more sinister reasons.

Many hotels have certainly tried to provide security. Sophisticated "magnetic" keys and access cards that can be re-programmed daily have replaced conventional keys in some larger hotels. Security cameras monitor entrances, hallways, elevators and lobby areas. Armed security guards patrol parking garages and hallways. Yet intruders manage to circumvent such precautions routinely.

The problem of crime in hotels is compounded by the fact that most people get a false sense of security from being in a hotel. Ellie Daniels never imagined that crime was such a problem in hotels. She was more concerned about fires. Had Ellie realized the danger, she would not have opened the door for Derek without first calling the front desk to confirm that a maintenance man was being sent to her room.

Ellie also would not have opened the door without first checking the peep-hole, which most hotel room doors have. Speaking through the closed, locked door, she would have asked the man to produce some identification proving he was a hotel employee. Only when she was satisfied he was actually a hotel maintenance man would she have admitted him.

As an extra measure of caution, Ellie would not have answered the door in her bathrobe. She would have slipped on her clothes. Then when the man stepped inside, she would have propped open the door, stepped out into the hallway and waited there until the man finished checking the smoke alarm. The idea is not to get trapped where there is no avenue of escape.

An even more prudent thing would have been for Ellie to call the front desk and request another room—one where the smoke alarm was functioning without need for repairs.

Once Derek was inside the room with the door locked behind him, he had Ellie perfectly positioned for the attack. Even a woman's screams often go unheard or unnoticed in hotel rooms. With a gun pointed at her face, Ellie had little choice but to give in and comply with the assailant's demands. The injury she received when she attempted to fight back illustrates the danger inherent in trying to deal with an armed attacker at close range. The best way to avoid becoming a victim is to be extremely cautious about every situation, no matter how innocent it might seem.

How to Keep It from Happening to You.

1. Never assume you are completely safe in your hotel room. A false sense of security could make you a victim of crime. Inquire about the hotel's security procedures before you check in. If you aren't convinced you are safe, you may be better off trying to find another hotel.

2. Always lock your hotel room from the inside and keep it locked the entire time you are in your room. Use every lock on the door. All those locks wouldn't be there if they weren't needed.

3. If someone claiming to be on the hotel staff calls your room or knocks on your door without your having requested a service, call the front desk immediately. Never open the door to such a person until you have confirmed his or her reason for being there. If you have even the slightest suspicion, call the front desk and demand that hotel security be sent to investigate.

4. If you have ordered a service, do not open the door until you have looked through the peep-hole to check out the person at the door. Most hotel personnel wear uniforms and/or identification badges. If you don't recognize the person at the door, don't open it. Call the front desk and tell them your concerns. Demand that someone from hotel security be sent to investigate.

5. Lock all your cash, jewelry, credit cards, airline tickets and other valuables in the hotel safe. Check with the front desk to determine if the hotel has a safe place to check cameras, camcorders or laptop computers. If not, you're probably better off taking them with you each time you leave your room.

6. If you are traveling by car, unload your car when you stop at a motel for the night. Try to park your car in a well-lighted place. If possible, park near your room within earshot of car tampering.

7. Never leave anything of value in your car at hotels where you have to leave the car key with a parking attendant. If you read the fine print on the back of most claim checks, you'll notice that the hotel disclaims all responsibility for anything left in your car. There's good reason for such disclaimers.

8. Carry a portable smoke and intrusion alarm along on your travels, and use it while you are in your hotel room.

9. Carry a portable travel lock for additional security on your hotel room door.

10. Never be reluctant to call the front desk or hotel security to report something suspicious. If it turns out to be a false alarm, so much the better. Remember, you have every right to DEMAND adequate security at your hotel.

1:36 p.m., Philadelphia, Pennsylvania

Mary Milken took the down elevator in her office tower building in Philadelphia, thinking about the meeting with the attorneys at Brown, Barfield and Barrows to discuss a tax problem with one of her clients. Mary abhorred lengthy, unproductive meetings with boring lawyers.

She glanced at her reflection in the mirrored elevator doors, patted her short stylish brunette hair and tugged slightly at the skirt of her navy blue suit. Her appearance was neat and professional, an image that clearly depicted her personality.

Being a certified public accountant, Mary Milken was always heavily laden with files, computer runs and various reports for her clients. Today was no different. After her meeting with the attorneys downtown, she had to deliver quarterly returns to her largest account, Bishop Industries. The elevator ride down ended in the basement where she had to exit and make her way to the entry of the nine-story parking garage next door.

While waiting for the garage elevator that would take her up to the sixth floor and her BMW, Mary looked at her watch. It was already 1:30 which meant she would have to call the attorneys from her car phone and let them know she would be late. While impatiently tapping her foot and staring at the closed polished elevator doors, a tall man dressed in a business suit studied Mary. Based on appearances, the good-looking, well-dressed man would not have warranted concern. Mary Milken was about to learn just how deceiving appearances can be.

The man had been arrested in Miami, Florida, in 1968, for statutory rape, receiving probation. Three years later in Memphis, Tennessee, he was arrested for sexual assault, but the charges were dropped by the complainant. In 1987, he was convicted for raping a 61-year-old grandmother in Reading, Pennsylvania, and served three years of a 15-year sentence. And now, Robert Summers was looking for another victim, someone not paying attention, distracted, unprepared for an attack. Mary Milken was perfect.

"Finally," Mary Milken blurted out as the elevator doors slid open. Mary waited for the people on board to file out then entered the elevator. Before the doors closed four well-dressed women and Robert Summers got on the elevator for the ascent to the upper floors of the parking garage. Robert Summers pushed the button for the seventh floor.

The elevator stopped on the sixth floor and Mary hurried out. She twisted her left wrist around in an attempt to see her watch and check the time once again. However, the motion of twisting her wrist caused her to drop the files in her hand. Angrily, she stooped over and began collecting the papers strewn on the dirty garage floor.

Robert Summers got off the elevator on the seventh floor and hurried to the stairs. Taking two steps at a time, he went down to the sixth floor and quietly opened the door. He didn't see Mary and wondered how she could have gotten in her car so quickly.

"Dammit!" Mary screamed as she dropped another file. "Damn, damn, damn."

"Thank you very much. I thought I had lost you," Robert Summers whispered to himself.

With the files firmly in hand, Mary stood up and walked in the general direction of her BMW. She resented the fact that, unlike most of her peers, she didn't have an assigned parking space. Consequently, she'd have to search for her car instead of walking directly to it. "Damn," she muttered to herself as she looked first to her right and then to her left. Mary wondered for a second if she might have parked on another floor this morning. It also occurred to her to find her car keys in her purse and hit the alarm button. She could just follow the alarm blasts to her car. But then she spotted her car.

Discreetly circling her like a shark watching a wounded fish was Robert Summers. He had yet another advantage. He had found a document near the elevator that could be used as a device to walk right up to the unsuspecting victim. So far, Robert thought, the woman was making all the right mistakes.

The BMW was parked in a dark corner of the garage. The recessed light directly above the car had been out for about a week. Maintenance was scheduled to replace the bulb later in the day. Robert Summers watched as Mary laid her armload of files on the hood of the car and began rummaging through her purse to find the keys. Robert Summers smelled blood and moved in for the kill.

"Excuse me," he called. "Mam?"

Mary Milken jerked her head up as if she had been slapped. "Yes?" she replied cautiously.

He held out the document so Mary could see it. "This was lying on the floor next to the elevator. I thought it might be one of yours," Robert said as he took several steps toward Mary. He wanted to see how she was going to react.

"Oh, thanks," she said with a secret sigh of relief. She held out her hand to take the document. Robert closed in with a smile of anticipation. He knew she was his for the taking, now.

"Here you go. Have a nice day," Robert said as he handed her the document.

"Thanks. You, too," Mary replied.

Assuming that was the end of the conversation, Mary returned her attention to finding the keys in her purse. As she was rooting around in the purse, her compact popped out and fell on the floor. "Dammit!"

"Here, let me help you. You seem to be having problems juggling all this," he said smoothly. Before she could respond, Robert scooped the compact and laid it on the hood with his left hand. With his right hand, he grabbed her by the throat and placed all of his weight against her. Caught totally off guard, Mary lost her balance and fell between the car and the wall of the garage. Robert immediately clasped his left hand over her mouth before she could scream. With his right hand, he reached into his coat pocket and took out a green silk scarf. Deftly, he held Mary in place and managed to get the scarf around her neck. He twisted the scarf twice very quickly, applying pressure to Mary's throat. She clawed at the scarf, but stopped when he spoke.

"Do you wanna die?"

Mary shook her head, her deep brown eyes showing abject terror.

"Good," he replied as he twisted the scarf a little tighter. "Then don't make me angry."

He told her to pull her panty hose and panties down. She hesitated. He removed his left hand from her mouth knowing that, with the scarf choking her, it would be difficult for her to scream. He unzipped the front of his trousers.

"I'm on my period," she whispered, obviously not wanting to make him angry.

Robert ignored her. Many women had used that line, as well as, "I've got AIDS...I'm a virgin...I've got Herpes," and on and on. He didn't care. It wasn't the sex that mattered to Robert Summers. It was the domination, the complete control that he wanted.

Mary realized that any second he was going to lift her skirt and see that she had lied about her period. Her mind worked through her options frantically. Finally, she decided. Mustering all of her strength, she shoved him. The hand holding the scarf relaxed, but only momentarily. She tried to roll underneath the car to escape. However, Robert quickly tightened his grip on the scarf, preventing her from getting more than an arm's length away. Using the scarf as a tether, he reeled her back to him. With both hands, he tightened the scarf around her neck.

Mary Milken's mind told her to fight or die. She didn't want to die—couldn't die—not now, not with the meetings this afternoon, not on the floor of some filthy garage, not...she lost consciousness.

Three days later, the police asked Mary Milken to come downtown to view several suspects in a line-up. She closely scrutinized each of the seven men. As she did so, Mary kept hearing the voice whispering in her ear, "Do you wanna die? Then don't make me angry." When she spotted Robert Summers in the line-up, a jolt of fear riveted her to the wooden chair she was sitting in. Her fear was so strong that she couldn't bring herself to lift a hand and point to him. Her mind screamed at her to lift her hand, point the finger, identify her rapist, but she couldn't do it. Mary simply looked away and shook her head "no."

Now, Mary Milken lives in fear every minute of the day. For all she knows, Robert Summers is still out there. If not Summers, someone just as bad or even worse.

Robert Summers' rape of Mary Milken was the tenth of 17 women he would rape before being caught and sent to prison where he now is serving a 12-year sentence.

Survival Analysis

Mary Milken didn't know it, but she made just about every mistake in the book as she walked through the parking garage on the day of her attack. Of course, Mary Milken shouldn't have had to worry about being raped in broad daylight in the parking garage. She was an honest citizen going about her business in the course of what seemed like just any other day, confident and unafraid.

Like so many of the cases we analyze, Mary Milken's rape might possibly have been avoided had she been alert to the dangers she faced. Parking garages by their very nature are spooky places and should elicit a degree of caution from anyone who uses them. There are all sorts of hiding places for assailants behind parked cars and pillars, even in stair wells and elevators. Garages also are usually dimly lit. And during normal working hours when most people are in their offices, there are few people around.

As Robert Summers noted, Mary Milken made all the right mistakes that tragic day. To begin with, she was preoccupied with getting to her meeting. She wasn't concentrating on the task at hand: getting safely to her car. Had Mary been more aware of the danger she faced, she would have known precisely where her car was parked. Also, she would have had her car keys in her hand. The objective is to get to your car as quickly as possible, and get inside and lock the door behind you. It also would have been helpful if Mary had secured her files (either in a box or a brief-case) before she left her office. Had she seemed less preoccupied and more certain about her actions, Robert Summers might not have targeted her as she waited for the elevator. Also, if she had walked briskly to her car after getting off the elevator, Summers might have been too late to catch up with her.

There was little reason for Mary to be suspicious of Summers as he approached her with the document in his hand. After all, she had dropped one of her files as she got off the elevator. And he was dressed in a business suit as though he belonged in the parking garage. The subterfuge had the desired effect in that Mary dropped her guard. Here again, we don't mean to suggest that every stranger be viewed with suspicion, but certainly with a degree of wariness. Remember, too, that Mary's car was parked in a dark corner of the garage. Once he handed the document to her, she never should have taken her eyes off him until he stepped away, assuming that he might have done so.

Had she been watching him cautiously, she might not have been caught off guard by his attack. At the very least, she might have been able to scream, which possibly would have frightened Summers away. As it turned out, Mary Milken was lucky. She lived to tell about it. But too fearful to tell it all.

How to Keep It from Happening to You.

1. Always try to park in a well-lighted section of a parking garage, and make a mental note of exactly where you park (if necessary, write it down). The more time you spend wandering around a parking garage looking for your car, the more of a target you become.

2. Be aware of the fact that enclosed parking garages provide plenty of cover for a possible attacker, so be alert the entire time you are there.

3. Keep your car keys in your hand when going to and from your car. If you have to get inside the car for safety, you won't have to fumble around for the key.

4. Check out the scene as you drive up to your parking space. If you feel uncomfortable about the situation, don't get out of your car. Return to the garage entrance and report it to the attendant.

5. Never stop to answer questions of a stranger. If someone stops his vehicle to ask for information, keep a safe distance between yourself and the stranger's car. If the driver or a passenger makes an overt move toward you—or makes any kind of sexual innuendo—leave as quickly as possible. If possible, return to the building and alert security. Or get inside your car and lock the door behind you. If necessary, lean on the horn to attract attention.

6. If you are confronted by an attacker and can't get to the building or inside your car, try to keep a parked car between you and the attacker as a buffer, all the while screaming at the top of your lungs. If the attacker demands your purse or wallet, comply by tossing it to him over the car. It is better to give up possessions than to risk a physical assault.

7. Try to avoid walking alone in parking garage stairwells. They're often dimly lit and somewhat isolated. If there's no one else around, you're probably safer walking up or down the auto ramp where you at least have a field of vision that might enable you to see someone approaching. You also have a better escape route on the ramp than you do in the stairwell. And if you have to scream, you're more likely to be heard out in the open than inside an enclosed stairwell.

8. Unless you work in a very secure building, it's a good idea to avoid stairwells altogether. Although some people routinely use stairwells for exercise, most people don't, so stairwells are usually pretty lonely places. Also, while you can usually

enter the stairwell from any floor inside the building, you can't always re-enter the building on every floor. Therefore, if you're attacked in a stairwell, you might have to run up or down several flights of stairs to reach an avenue of escape.

9. Be equally cautious in parking garage elevators. Make it a habit to stand as close as possible to the floor selection buttons. If someone threatens you, press the elevator alarm button. Also, press as many floor buttons as you can. That will cause the elevator to stop on several floors, increasing your chances of getting help.

10. Make it a habit to carry a purse-size canister of chemical protection spray in the palm of your hand each time you go to and from your parked car. It's an extra measure of protection that just might save your life.

2:45 p.m., Las Vegas, Nevada

The housing market in Las Vegas was almost as hot as the blistering heat. Jeanell Anderson had never known it to get this hot so early in the year. But as long as home buyers kept coming through the doors in record numbers, she wasn't complaining.

Jeanell was one of the top performing real estate agents in Las Vegas. She had already sold more than a million dollars worth of real estate, and the year wasn't half over. Of course, she had to work an average of 12 hours a day, seven days a week to do it. It seemed like she never had time of her own. With a car phone in her red Seville, a business phone at home, an office phone and voice mail with a pager, she spent practically every waking hour talking about real estate, showing real estate or closing real estate sales.

Jeanell had several things going for her. She was very ambitious and worked tirelessly to be a success. She had gone into real estate out of necessity following her divorce five years ago, having recognized the profession as being one where she wouldn't be held back because she was female. In residential real estate, you're limited only by your drive and determination. Jeanell, who was in her late thirties, was also very attractive, a virtue she played to the hilt. She had a way about her that men found sexy, yet she wasn't intimidating to other women. Finally, Jeanell understood the value of advertising and promotion. Every Sunday, she ran a half-page ad in the local newspaper touting her sales abilities. A photo of her smiling face was a dominant element of every advertisement and promotional flyer she did.

Alex Creighton had first seen her picture in an advertisement back in December. It was obsession at first sight. He saw her ad again the following week, and the week after that. Alex knew he had to have her and began formulating a plan.

Alex was 29 years old. He had come to Las Vegas eight years earlier after leaving the University of Iowa in the middle of his junior year. Alex had been accused of date rape by a female student, and rather than waiting for formal charges to be filed, he droppped out of school and left town. He had hoped to make it as a stand-up comedian. But he had never made it beyond dealing blackjack at the Purple Sage Casino. His shift from midnight to eight a.m. gave him plenty of time during the day to follow through with his plans for Jeanell.

Early in February, Alex called Jeanell to inquire about several of the homes she had listed. He identified himself as Doctor Michael Pittman, from Davenport, Iowa. He indicated that he was in town looking for a home prior to relocating to Las Vegas in the spring. Jeanell was more than happy to show him some of the property she had listed, and they made an appointment to meet at Jeanell's office later that day. The standard procedure

was to have a prospect meet in her office, make a copy of the
prospect's driver's license and leave it with the receptionist when
she left to show property. It was an extra measure of safety most
real estate professionals had started using as a safeguard against
rape and robbery. It was something Alex hadn't expected.

When Alex arrived for his two o'clock appointment, he was
beside himself with anticipation. Her voice on the phone had
been mesmerizing, and he had been fantasizing about her ever
since. When she stepped out of her office to greet him, Alex
knew that one way or another he had to have her. "God, she's
even more gorgeous in person," he thought to himself. Something
electrifying happened to Alex when she shook his hand and
introduced herself. If there had ever been any doubts about his
plan, they were immediately dispelled. She would be his, one
way or the other.

They spent several minutes discussing the various neighborhoods in Las Vegas. When it was time to go look at some of the
houses, Jeanell asked Alex for his driver's license, explaining it
was standard procedure. Alex quickly concocted a story about
having left his wallet back at the hotel. He explained that he had
to catch a plane back home later that same day, and that he didn't
have time to return to the hotel for his wallet.

At first, Jeanell was dubious about leaving the office with
Alex, but he seemed harmless enough. He was clean-cut, well-
dressed, even handsome. She hated to let a prospect slip away, so
she decided to go ahead and leave with him in spite of the fact he
didn't have identification. They spent the next two hours looking
at houses in an expensive neighborhood north of the city. Alex
wasn't looking at the houses, though. Alex was looking for the
right opportunity. Fortunately for Jeanell, it never presented itself.
There was one brief moment when he considered making his

move on her. However, the owners of the house were due back within the hour, and he needed longer than that to savor Jeanell. Alex was convinced the right opening would present itself. He just had to be patient.

Over the next several months, the scenario was repeated every week or so. It wasn't long before Jeanell had totally dropped her guard. She fully believed that Alex was who he said he was, and that he wanted nothing more than to find the right house for his needs. In fact, she had even come to enjoy his company. He was young, good- looking and, judging from the price range of homes he was considering, was fairly affluent. Still, it wouldn't be very professional to become romantically involved with a client, so she pushed any such thoughts out of her mind. What she really wanted to do was find this guy a house. She had a sizable amount of time invested in Alex and wanted to sell him a house to make up for some of it. She had no idea of the sick game Alex was playing. She wouldn't find out until one afternoon in April.

At 11:30 a.m. that morning, Alex called to tell Jeanell he had driven by a house with acreage for sale about 15 miles outside Las Vegas. He asked Jeanell to make an appointment to show him the house at 2:00 that afternoon. He had already checked out the house and knew it was vacant. At long last, the perfect opportunity was about to open for Alex.

When Jeanell turned onto the road leading up to the house, she saw Alex standing in the shade of the front porch. "I hope you haven't been waiting long," she said as she got out of her car. "This heat is unbearable."

"Oh, well, I've got to get used to it if I'm going to live in Las Vegas," he said good naturedly. "This house looks perfect from the outside. If the price is right, this may finally be it."

"They're asking three-fifty, but I think we can get them down off that," she said as she took the door key out of the lock box and opened the front door. A blast of cool air struck them as they went inside.

"Thank goodness they left the air conditioner running," Jeanell said.

"It feels great in here," Alex said as he walked into the kitchen. He nodded his head affirmatively as he went from room to room on the first floor. Jeanell thought he was hooked.

"Looks great down here," Alex said. "Let's have a look at the upstairs." He stepped aside to let her lead the way up the stairs. As he watched her hips sway from side to side as she moved up the stairs ahead of him, he was tempted to reach out and squeeze her buttocks. But he held back.

They went into several rooms on the second floor, stopping in the middle of the huge master bedroom. Alex nodded his head and said, "Yeah, this is the one."

"Great," Jeaneall replied. "We'll go back and draw up the contract."

"What, no celebration?" Alex asked as he stepped toward her. "The least you could do is help me break in the bedroom."

Jeanell thought he was reaching out to shake her hand. Instead, he grabbed her roughly around the waist and pulled her to him. "A little afternoon delight would do us both good."

"Get your hands off me!" Jeanell demanded as she tried to push him away.

"Uh-uh, no way, pretty lady," Alex said as he ran his free hand up between her legs. "I mean to have me a little of this, right here and now."

Jeanell struggled to push away from him, but Alex tightened his grip on her waist. "Stop, I mean it, you bastard. This isn't part of the deal," Jeanell said angrily.

Alex just laughed and began roughly working his fingers inside her panties. "Goddamit, stop!" she screamed as she dropped her purse and began punching at Alex. He suddenly pulled his hand from between her legs, and backhanded her with great force across the side of her face. The blow struck fear in Jeanell as she fell backward. Alex stepped forward and continued to backhand her until she dropped to the floor sobbing hysterically.

"We can do this the easy way or the hard way. It's up to you," Alex said as he took off his coat and began removing his tie and shirt. "What'll it be?" he asked as he stood over her with his bare chest exposed.

Jeanell rubbed at her swollen lip, and stopped suddenly as she saw the blood on her hand. Alex grabbed her by the hair and pulled her head back. "Hard or easy?" as he pulled her head back further.

"Easy," she replied meekly. "I'll do anything...just don't hurt me," she said through broken sobs.

"Too late. You lost your choice. We'll just have to do it my way," Alex said as he began removing his belt. He leaned down and started ripping at Jeanell's dress and bra. "Besides, you've been a very bad girl, teasing old Alex all these months with that cute little ass of yours. Now, I'm gonna have to spank it."

Alex stripped her naked, and using her panty hose as a cord, tied her hands to a doorknob. He then began to beat her back side with the belt. Her screams and pleas only heightened his pleasure. She was whipped, raped and sodomized by Alex off and on for the next six hours. At 10:00 that evening, Alex left her there still tied to the doorknob. Before leaving, he warned Jeanell that if she reported the incident to the police, he would come back and kill her.

About a half hour after Alex had left, Jeanell worked herself free, went to her car phone and called the police. Even though Jeanell was able to provide a good description of her assailant, Alex Creighton has never been apprehended.

A few days later, Alex left his job at the casino. Although his whereabouts are unknown, he continues to call and terrorize Jeanell. She now carries a gun in her purse and keeps her hand on it the entire time she is showing property to a prospect.

Survival Analysis

Jeanell Anderson was the victim of one of the most terrifying and unpredictable criminal personalities: a person who has an obsessive attraction to his victim. Sometimes, as in the case of Jeanell Anderson, the victim will be stalked for months and set up for an attack.

In a way, Alex Creighton felt a link with Jeanell, but it was hardly romantic. He obviously desired her sexually, but the viciousness of his attack seemed to indicate a deep-seated resentment of some sort.

Alex initially became transfixed on Jeanell by seeing her photograph in newspaper ads week after week. That was possibly Jeanell's first mistake. She was a very attractive woman, and Alex may have thought she was exploiting it by using it in advertisements. Of course, models, movie stars—even local TV news personalities—have built careers on looks alone. Many of these celebrities also become targets of stalkers. However, most of them have the protection of body guards or security guards to help keep the screwballs away. Jeanell didn't have that luxury. She had to go out every day in the presence of strangers, sometimes to vacant or unoccupied houses where she was extremely vulnerable.

Probably the last thing Jeanell should have done was to use her photograph in an ad, especially in light of her good looks. The more visible a person is, the more likely he or she is to attract an Alex Creighton. Sadly, being inconspicuous is a self-defense technique in this day and age.

Of course, Jeanell should not have violated the rule about showing property without meeting the prospective buyer at her office and having the prospect leave a photocopy of his driver's license there. Following this procedure might have kept her from being attacked. It offers a degree of protection for people like real estate agents, since it provides a record of who they are with and what the person looks like. It would deter most rapists since they know they could easily be identified.

However, even such a safeguard shouldn't have kept Jeanell from carrying a self-defense weapon. Here again, we cite the advantage of a powerful chemical spray like The Protector. It might have kept her from being raped and beaten. Had she been alert to the danger of rape (as any woman should be when she is alone with a stranger), Jeanell would never have let Alex get close enough for the attack. She would have had the chemical spray in her hand (it attaches to a key ring) as she walked through the house with Alex. Furthermore, she would always have let Alex go into each room ahead of her, so that he couldn't grab her from behind or block the doorway to prevent her escape.

All this may sound like more paranoia. But it's really just exercising a high degree of caution. Remember, it's a lot more difficult for someone to attack you if you're ready for it.

This also may sound like blame is being placed on Jeanell for what happened, but that's not the intent. Even with all the mistakes she made, she is totally blameless for the attack. She simply didn't think it could ever happen to her. But she's certainly not alone in that respect. Probably 99% of all crime victims never thought it would happen to them either.

How to Keep It from Happening to You.

1. If you're in a profession that brings you in contact with strangers, stay alert. It is possible to be polite and personable and still be cautious.

2. Don't take unnecessary risks. If your company has personal safety procedures, follow them religiously. They were probably created out of necessity.

3. Try to be as inconspicuous as possible. Wearing expensive clothes and jewelry or driving a flashy car could easily make you the target of a robber.

4. Make sure someone knows where you are, and whenever possible, who you're with every time you go out on an appointment or sales call. If you have a cellular phone, use it to stay in touch with your office.

5. If you travel, be careful in your hotel room. Many thieves and rapists get into hotel rooms with keys they deliberately do not return when checking out. A portable smoke and intrusion alarm is a good thing to take along on out of town trips. So is a portable travel lock for extra security on your hotel room door.

6. Carry a personal defense device such as a canister of The Protector. But don't let it give you a false sense of security. The best way to avoid being a victim is to stay alert to the possibilities of being victimized at all times.

3:45 p.m., Atlanta, Georgia.

Kelly Williams and Jennifer Keats had first met as 10-year-olds on the neighborhood swim team. The chemistry between the two was amazing, and they instantly became best friends. They both found it incredible that they had so much in common. They liked the same clothes, had the same taste in food, and worshipped their same favorite singer, Madonna. In fact, both girls carefully followed the latest fashion trends set by Madonna and did their best to emulate her—pushing their parents restrictions to the limit. They both had dreams of someday becoming singers like Madonna. On the nights when one or the other would sleep over, they'd be awake all night lip-syncing and dancing to Madonna's latest album or music video.

By the age of 13, Kelly and Jennifer had undergone the change from childhood to adolescence. The only similarity between their lives as 10-year-olds and now was their idolatry of Madonna. Now, the two girls spent every spare moment their parents would allow cruising the stores and checking out the guys at Westbrook Mall, a sprawling complex in an affluent suburb northwest of Atlanta, Georgia. Usually the mall was off-limits on school days, but today was an exception. A school dance was just a few days away, and since the Williams family was going to be out of town this coming weekend, Kelly had nagged her mother into letting her go to the mall today after school to look for a dress.

It was 3:30 p.m. when Cindy Williams dropped off her daughter and Jennifer at Westbrook Mall with the usual warning, "Don't you dare leave this mall for any reason," followed with, "I'll pick you up right here at 5:30...don't be late."

Kelly slammed the door angrily and the two went into the mall. "That kid," Cindy thought to herself, "is really turning into a brat." Almost overnight, her cute, sweet little girl had turned into a rude, difficult little snip. Cindy guessed it was pretty typical for an adolescent, but she never imagined adolescence came so quickly, or could be quite so trying.

"God, your mother is such a bore," Jennifer said to Kelly as they walked away from the car.

"Totally," Kelly replied.

"So is mine," Jennifer said. "She's always nagging about my hair, or clothes, or grades or something."

"God, I hate that, don't you?" Kelly replied as they made their way through the sparse crowd at in mall.

"Totally," Jennifer said, as she pulled out a package of cigarettes hidden in her purse. She offered one to Kelly, and they both awkwardly lit up and took a drag. Neither inhaled, and they both hated the way it tasted. But they thought it made them look sexy. After all, Madonna smokes!

"Oh my God," look at that cute guy with the long hair," Jennifer said suddenly.

"Where?" Kelly asked.

"Up there, he's coming this way. He is so fine!" Jennifer said as Kelly craned her neck to look.

"Don't look, dummy, he'll see you," Jennifer said.

"Yuuk! That guy! He's old," Kelly said as she spied Pete Kluge.

"He is so fine," Jennifer said as Pete got closer.

"He is kind of cute," Kelly said after getting a closer look at the handsome 22-year-old sauntering toward them.

"God, it's Bon Jovi!" Jennifer said with a giggle.

Pete Kluge did bear a slight resemblance to the rock star. He had long, flowing brownish blond hair, a perfect tan and a face that could easily have been chiseled by a sculptor. Dressed in jeans and a pale blue cotton shirt, he looked like he might have just stepped out of a J. Crew catalog. A brown leather pouch was slung over his arm, and an expensive looking Minolta camera was hanging around his neck.

When he was about ten feet from the girls, he quickly brought the camera up to his eye and said to them, "Hold it right there, ladies," then clicked the shutter. The motor-drive on the camera fired off five shots as the startled but very flattered girls looked at one another and giggled.

Pete then reached in his shirt pocket and took out a business card. "Ladies, allow me to introduce myself. Pete Kluge, talent scout of the stars," he said with a good natured smile that nearly melted the two girls.

Kelly nervously took the card from Pete as he continued, "I'm out here today scouting locations for a new video we're shooting," he said.

"Which one?" Jennifer asked excitedly.

"I can't say right now...we don't want the publicity until we decide on the location...but I can tell you, it's for a really big star."

"Madonna?" Kelly asked.

"Well...you never know," Pete replied trying to be coy enough to hold their interest.

"Oh my God!" Jennifer squealed, "I would just die if it was Madonna."

"Totally die," Kelly said.

"Could we watch?" Jennifer asked excitedly.

"Even better. You might get to be in it. We need a few extras for some of the shots."

"Oh my God. Wouldn't Heather just die if she saw us on MTV," Jennifer shrieked.

"Totally die," Kelly said.

"I gather you don't care for Heather," Pete said.

"God, we hate her," Jennifer replied.

"Well, we won't let Heather be in the video, then," Pete said in amusement. "If we decide to use you, we'll need your parents' consent...assuming you're under 18," Pete said to flatter the girls.

"We're both 16," Jennifer lied.

"More like 12," Pete thought to himself as he reached into his brown leather pouch and took out two official looking model release forms, "and so much the better."

"You'll need to get your parents to sign this form," Pete said as he handed one to each girl.

"When will it be?" Kelly asked as she glanced at the form.

"In just a few days," Pete replied, "while the singer is in town for a concert."

"Oh my God!" the two girls squealed. Madonna herself was scheduled to do a concert in Atlanta next week. Of course, neither girl's parents would permit them to attend the concert. Wouldn't it be awesome if they got to see her in person in spite of their parents. It had to be a Madonna video they were shooting.

Of course, Pete knew that Madonna would be in town, too. The girls were thinking just the way he figured. The girls had taken the bait. Now all he had to do was reel them in.

"Don't get your hopes up too high. We're interviewing about a hundred girls...and we only need six," Pete cautioned.

"When do the interviews start?" Jennifer asked.

"They've already started. We have a production office over at the Raddison Hotel," he replied. "How soon can you get your consent forms signed?" he asked.

"Not till tonight," Jennifer said as Kelly shook her head in wide-eyed agreement.

"Hmmm, tomorrow might be too late," Pete said. "Do you feel pretty confident your parents will let you do it?"

"For sure! Right!" the two girls answered.

"I'll tell you what, I'm on my way back over to the production office now. You could follow me over there, have your interview, and then get your parents to sign. They'll probably be more likely to let you do it if they know you already have the part," Pete said.

"Uh...we don't have a car here. My mom dropped me off," Kelly said in embarrassment. Of course, Pete Kluge knew they were too young to be driving a car.

Pete was smooth. He had done this many times before in cities all across the southeast. There was a big market for young girls and boys for prostitution rings throughout the world, and Pete was one of hundreds of suppliers. Blonde-haired, blue-eyed girls fetched a premium price, with a big bonus for virgins. He figured Kelly and Jennifer would net him at least $10,000 after expenses. The money was all but his.

"Well, I guess I could drive you over...if you think it would be okay with your mom. I don't want to do anything to get you in trouble," he said.

"My mom would kill me," Kelly said sternly to Jennifer.

"Kelly!" Jennifer whined. "Come on, she won't mind. We'll be back before she picks us up. She won't even know we went."

"What time is she picking you up?" Pete asked.

"5:30," Kelly said dejectedly.

"Hey, it's only 3:45 now," Pete said as he glanced at his watch. "We can be over there and back in an hour," Pete lied.

"Come on, Kelly. Don't you want to be in a video? With Madonna!" Jennifer exhorted.

"Sure, I want to...but...you really think it would be okay?" she asked Jennifer as her resistance started to fade.

"I'm sure!" Jennifer said emphatically.

"Great. Let's go so we can be sure to be back before your mom gets here," Pete said as he gestured toward the exit.

Kelly, against her better judgement, left with Jennifer and Pete. They drove away from the mall in Pete's red Mustang with dark tinted windows. No one saw them leave. Kelly and Jennifer have never been seen or heard from since.

Survival Analysis

The case of Kelly Williams and Jennifer Keats, like the case of Sean Matthews (see page 113) is another terrifying reminder of how vulnerable our children are to the criminals that prey on them. There were Kelly and Jennifer, two perfectly normal young teen-age girls, in an upscale mall in an affluent part of town, both of whom had been warned about leaving the mall with anyone for any reason—and yet they were lured away by Pete Kluge with amazing ease.

Remember, though, although teen-agers are striving to assert their independence, they are still very naive and easily won over by a disarming stranger with an attractive lure or scheme. In some ways, teen-agers are at greater risk than younger children, since they are often rebelling against parental authority, leading them to do things out of defiance. Also, it is sometimes difficult for parents to communicate with adolescents, so ideally, children should start receiving proper training in the dangers of molesta-tion and exploitation before their teen-age years.

Both Jennifer and Kelly would have been much less vulner-able to Pete had they known something about the modus operandi of abductors. They troll areas commonly frequented by young people. Shopping malls and video arcades are two places they often find them.

Molesters and abductors somehow manage to captivate their prey with concocted stories about something of interest. Once a molester gets a kid enthused about the possibility of doing or seeing something of particular interest, he is then able to convince the kid to leave the premises with him. Molesters usually are masters of deceit, and under the right circumstances can spirit a victim away in a matter of minutes.

Of course, Kelly's mother thought she had made herself perfectly clear when she told Kelly and Jennifer not to leave the mall under any circumstances. But as we have already stated, warnings are not enough. Had Kelly's and Jennifer's parents acted out various scenarios involving common lures used by child abductors, both girls would have been better prepared when they encountered Pete Kluge.

They would have known that the proper thing to do was to politely decline to talk to the stranger. Then they would have continued walking down the mall away from the stranger. If the stranger had persisted in his efforts, the girls would have become more forceful in their refusal. If the stranger had persisted even further, they would have known that the proper thing to do at that point was to find a mall security officer and report the harassment. Even though the stranger's intentions might have been perfectly innocent, they would have had every right to alert security. Remember, it is better to risk being wrong than to risk your life.

How to Keep It from Happening to Your Kids

1. Role play with your children to teach them the techniques and lures used by child molesters and abductors. This should begin at an early age, before adolescence, when children are more receptive to communication with parents.

2. Teach your kids that they are never to accept gifts and favors from strangers under any circumstances. A polite but assertive refusal is the best way for kids to respond when offered such favors. Offers of fame, good-paying jobs, sex or drugs are lures most commonly used by abductors against adolescents.

3. Teach your kids that they absolutely never get into a car with a stranger if they have even the slightest doubt about the stranger's authority.

4. Continually reinforce such training by running through drills with your kids involving various scenarios. Try to turn the drill into a game so it seems less threatening to children. Remember, the objective is to enlighten, not frighten.

5. Have your kids fingerprinted, and have a set of prints on file where other family members know where they are kept.

6. Take photographs of your kids at least once a year. A recent photograph will come in very handy if one of your kids is ever missing. Keep several prints on hand. You'll need copies for the police, and possibly a copy to use in printing flyers to hand out in the area where the child disappeared.

7. Always know where your kids are, whom they are with and what clothing they are wearing. This information can be vital in starting a search if your child is missing.

8. Monitor the activities of your kids. Listen to their music. If you disapprove of the lyrics, or the actions or lifestyle of the singer, take action. It's not only your right, it's your responsibility. Kids are easily influenced by music, rock videos, movies and television shows.

9. Know the names, addresses and phone numbers of your child's friends. If possible, get a photograph from the friend's parents. Network with the parents as much as possible to keep a better pulse on what is going on with your children. Know their haunts and hang-outs. All this information can be vital if you're trying to locate a missing child.

10. If your child turns up missing, don't wait for the police to act. In some cities, police will not list a teen-ager as missing until he or she has been gone at least three days. By then, it may be too late. Immediately mobilize family, friends and neighbors to begin a search. Time is critical. THE AVERAGE LIFE EXPECTANCY OF AN ABDUCTED CHILD IS ONLY 14 TO 48 HOURS.

4:00 p.m., Washington, D.C.

W aleeb Attar didn't believe in fate. No, life to Waleeb was like a Seurat painting, carefully laid out in grids on the canvas, with each moment meticulously set into place like the dots in a pointilist painting. His family had begun planning his life even before his birth 26 years ago.

Waleeb's mother and father had come to America from India on a student visa. Waleeb had been born while his father was working on a Ph.D. in physics at Rice University in Houston, Texas. Even though Waleeb was an American citizen by birth, he was raised under the rigid structure of Indian family life. Everything he did followed the plans laid out by his father. When he was 10 years old, his marriage to Sasheen Rasha had been pre-arranged. As was the custom, both Waleeb and Sasheen would remain celibate until their marriage.

Maintaining his virginity hadn't been easy for Waleeb. After all, he had grown up in a sexually permissive society. Many of his peers lost their virginity in their early teens. All Waleeb could do was listen to their stories of sexual encounters and wonder what it must be like. Waleeb thought about it a lot.

When Waleeb was a student at the University of Houston, he spent what little free time he had frequenting the city's infamous topless bars. While sipping on a five-dollar soft drink, he would watch the dancers on stage and wonder about his bride to be. Although he had never seen her, never spoken a word to her, he lusted madly for Sasheen Rasha. The day of his marriage couldn't come soon enough for Waleeb.

It would be two years following his graduation before the wedding date was set. After receiving his degree, Waleeb had taken a promising job with the Department of Commerce in Washington, D.C. Only then was it determined that he had the resources to support a bride and the children that would soon follow. No, Waleeb did not believe in fate, only well-laid plans. Unfortunately, the plan did not account for Webster Barkum.

Fate had played a heavy hand in Webster Barkum's life, and it had been none too kind. Webster had been born out of wedlock to a 15-year-old drug addict who had died of an overdose two years after his birth. He had spent the better part of his life in and out of foster homes, graduating to reform school when he was 11. By the time he turned 16, Webster's police record was a two-file volume in the Juvenile Division of the Washington D.C. police. Petty theft, assault with a deadly weapon, drug dealing, car theft, burglary—Webster had done it all, except for murder. That, too, would soon be added to his record.

It was 4:00 p.m. in Washington, D.C., when fate would bring Webster and Waleeb together for one brief moment in time. It was the day before his wedding to Sasheen.

Waleeb would normally be working in his office at the Commerce Department at this time of the afternoon. But he had scheduled his vacation to begin several days earlier in order to get everything ready for the wedding ceremony. Now he was on his way to the hotel where his family was staying to go over the last minute details of tomorrow's wedding. As he made his way through the traffic in his Accura, he could think only of Sasheen on their wedding night. He was so engrossed in his fantasy that he had to brake suddenly to avoid running a red light that had just changed from amber. He had gone partway into the crosswalk, so he put the car in reverse and turned to look behind him as he backed out of the crosswalk.

Ed Conway, in a Plymouth mini-van directly behind, was afraid Waleeb was going to back into him, so he gave a short beep on his horn. "You should have gone on through the light," Ed thought to himself as he nervously eyed Waleeb's car inching back. Ed was still a little irritated that Waleeb, in making a right turn on red, had turned in front of him several blocks back. Ed was in a big hurry to get back to his office. He had fabricated a story about a business meeting but had actually been at a hotel out by the airport, enjoying the company of Julia Fletcher whom he had met at a conference just two days earlier. Ed Conway never thought about fate one way or the other. But after the next few seconds of his life, he would think about it a lot.

When Waleeb turned his head back to the front, he saw the blur of Webster Barkum out of the corner of his eye. Suddenly, the driver's side door was wide open and Waleeb was looking down the barrel of Webster's .22 pistol.

"Out of the car, sucker, out of the car!" Webster shouted as he nervously looked at the other traffic on the street. "Out of the car, now, or I'm gonna kill your ass!"

"What do want?" Waleeb asked in confusion.

"I want your car. Get out now!" Webster shouted as he glanced around nervously.

"Why do...," Waleeb started to ask. He never finished the question.

Webster fired the gun point blank, hitting Waleeb between the eyes, killing him instantly. "I said out of the car," Webster shouted as he quickly reached in, popped Waleeb's seat belt and flung his body out into the street. Webster then jumped into the car, which started rolling forward when Waleeb's foot came off the brake, tore through the red light and disappeared into the Washington traffic.

Ed Conway was too stunned even to get the license number of Waleeb's car. It was broad daylight on a busy street in the nation's capital. How could such a thing be happening? It was like he was sitting in his living room watching a video. Ed Conway would remember it the rest of his life.

He would often wonder what might have happened if Waleeb Attar, the driver of the car in front of him, had sped up and gone through the amber light. Ed would have stopped for the red light. Would the assailant have come after his car? Would he have died then and there instead of Waleeb? Yeah, most likely, he'd be dead right now, he thought. He was glad he had spent that afternoon with Julia Fletcher. "You've got to enjoy yourself while you can," he thought. "You might not be around tomorrow." It just depends on what fate has in store.

Survival Analysis

Car jacking is a relatively new phenomenon in this country. Instead of stealing an unoccupied car, a thief will take the car right off the street while the driver is still inside. If the car doors are locked, the thief will often smash the window. Sometimes the driver is forced out of the car; other times, the driver is abducted when the car is taken. Car jackings occur at all hours of the day and night, in big cities and small, all across the nation.

Waleeb Attar wasn't really aware of this new wrinkle in car theft. Although it occurs on the average of three times a day in Washington, D.C. alone, it didn't get much attention on the news unless it resulted in a death. Waleeb never paid much attention to the reports.

Had Waleeb paid more attention to the news, he might have been more alert to the danger. But Waleeb was preoccupied with thoughts of his upcoming wedding. His mind definitely was not on his personal safety. He was so lost in thought that he nearly ran through an amber light that was turning red. Had he been concentrating on the road and what was happening around him, he might have been able to make it through the light without risking an accident.

When he stopped at the light and looked over his shoulder to back out of the crosswalk, he couldn't see what was going on to his left or right. Had he been on the alert, he probably would have seen Webster Barkum coming. When Webster started to open the door, he could have driven off, turning right at the red light. Also, had Waleeb's door been locked, Webster would have had a more difficult time getting to Waleeb to force him out of the car.

Of course, when Webster pulled the gun, Waleeb should have immediately complied with the command to get out of the car.

He should have done so without hesitating to ask questions.
When an assailant pulls a gun or knife, the safest thing you can
do is give up your property and do everything you can to survive.
Fighting, arguing or stalling can get you killed when facing a
panicky thief.

How to Keep It from Happening to You

1. If someone walks up to your car and tries to open the door for
   any reason, don't stop to ask questions. Drive away quickly
   but safely. Try not to panic and cause a traffic accident in the
   process.

2. Keep your windows rolled up and all doors locked when
   you're driving. If you need to have the windows rolled down
   for ventilation, crack them slightly, but not enough for
   someone to reach inside.

3. If someone approaches your car to ask for directions or
   assistance, don't roll down your window all the way. Crack it
   just enough to communicate.

4. When you pull up to a stop sign or red light, keep your car in
   gear.

5. Try to leave at least one full car length between your car and
   the car in front of you. By doing so, you won't be trapped
   without an escape route. If you see someone suspicious
   approaching your car, you will at least have room to maneuver and drive away. Try not to panic. Make sure the way is
   clear before you pull over into another lane of traffic to avoid
   being injured or killed in a car accident.

6. Keep your purse and other valuables out of sight while you're
   driving. If a thief doesn't see valuables in your car, he may
   not be as tempted.

7. If another car bumps you from the rear, be extremely cautious
    about getting out of your car to assess the damage. Look in
    your rear-view mirror first. Is the driver of the car that
    bumped you getting out of the car, or is it one of the passen-
    gers? If it's a passenger instead of the driver, the passenger
    could easily jump in your car and drive away while you're
    assessing the damage. If you feel the least bit suspicious,
    drive to a safe place, then get out and survey the damage.
    Report the incident to police. CAUTION: Don't leave the
    scene of an accident if it is serious or if an injury is involved.
    You could be charged with leaving the scene of an accident.
    If you have to remain at the scene, stay in your locked car if
    possible. However, if you can see that an injury is involved,
    you should render aid and call for help.

6:10 p.m., Seattle, Washington

The cool, crisp air was typical for Seattle in April. The clear blue sky wasn't. It hadn't rained in more than a week, and Sean Matthews was getting in as much time at the park as he possibly could. The heck with the Super Nintendo. The break in the dreary, wet weather was cause for celebration, not hibernation. Sean would join his two best friends, Mark and Sam, at the park next to Edison Elementary School, on North 45th Street only four blocks away.

The park was an open field cluttered with seesaws, swings, monkey bars, and a heavy gauge plastic tri-level fort that was great for a kid's fertile imagination. Riding his bike to the park, Sean thought about being a space pirate and attacking the mother ship skippered by Mark and defended by Sam. The excitement made Sean pedal the dirt bike a little faster.

As he approached the park, Sean squeezed the brake handles hard, bringing the bike to a screeching halt just off the blacktop parking lot. In his haste to meet with his friends, he'd forgotten to leave his mother a note—once again. That was twice this week. "She's gonna be mad," Sean thought to himself. "I better go back, or I'll get it when she gets home."

"Hey, Sean!"

"Over here, Sean."

He looked up to see both Mark and Sam on the fort waving toy swords at him. After only a moment's hesitation, Sean blistered a path directly to his friends. Sean decided that his mom would assume he was at the park, so why go all the way back home? Without realizing it, Sean Matthews had just decided between life and death.

At the very moment of that fateful decision, Tim Braverton stepped into the garage attached to his fashionable town house where he kept his newest and finest possession—a brand spanking new Corvette. It was silver with black interior and would run at speeds in excess of 150 mph with no strain at all. He was carrying a remote control toy replica of the Corvette, and had to fumble with it as he punched the button on the wall. The garage door swung open letting in the gloriously cool air from the outside. What a great day. If luck was with him, it would only get better.

Tim had left his office early and went home to change. He had a need this afternoon that couldn't be ignored any longer, and he knew exactly where to go to satisfy it. His need, which was as demanding as any need could be, wasn't for booze or drugs, not that either wouldn't be great afterwards; his need was more primal—Tim needed sex. Not wanted, needed, like a junkie needs a fix that will make him well for awhile.

Looking into the rear-view mirror, he caught a glimpse of himself and wondered what his father would think about all of this. It was, after all, his father who had introduced him to the world of perverted sex when he had been only seven. The first time had been just three months after his mother had died in a car accident, although Tim had faint memories of earlier, less overt sexual contact with his father long before that. In that first explicit encounter, his father had come to his bed and fondled him, explaining that it was all right for people who loved each other to do such things together. Tim would later tell how his father had continuously assaulted him even through his teen-age years and how he had come to accept such actions as being normal. Deep down inside, though, Tim felt nothing but revulsion for his father—and himself.

Tim Braverton had been caught only once. He had received probation from the judge because it was his first offense. He laughed to himself at that one. That was the first time he had been caught, yes, but it certainly wasn't his first offense. During his two-year probation, Tim had somehow managed to keep his urges under control, but they were still there none the less. It was during this time that Tim had become a model-car enthusiast, knowing full well that such an enticing novelty attracted young boys like the light attracts a moth. And once he was out from under the scrutiny of the court, he used his model cars as a lure for numerous young victims.

In the last six months alone, he had sexually assaulted eight young boys, being careful to do it in towns outside Seattle so as not to establish a pattern. More recently, though, he hadn't been having much luck, and his need was so strong that he couldn't wait for a trip out of town. Tim had been casing the neighbor-hood the past few days and had noticed Sean at the park about the same time each day.

The most troubling aspect of Tim's behavior lately was that the violence associated with each encounter had grown in intensity. The sex by itself was no longer completely fulfilling; in fact, it had become little more than foreplay. The physical abuse and torture afterwards was the climax.

Sean Matthews, the treacherous space pirate, made his third and final assault on the fortress guarded by Mark and Sam. This time, they wouldn't repulse him; this time he would destroy the fort and everyone inside. He screamed at the top of his lungs as he raced toward the enemy with his magical laser sword at the ready. It was a frightening, blood-curdling scream that caused others in the park to stop and look. They all continued to watch in mock terror as Sean attacked the plastic fort.

It was an epic battle that lasted a scant ten minutes before the three bored with the game. Mark and Sam decided it was time to leave, and in spite of Sean's pleading to stay and play something else, left for home.

But Sean wasn't ready to go yet. He guessed it would be at least an hour before his mother got home. She never arrived before 6:30, and he hated being there alone. That was the worst part of the divorce. Before his dad moved out last year, there was always somebody at home. Sean really missed having his dad around.

Sean scanned the nearly empty park for somebody else to play with. A teen-ager and his girlfriend smooching on the swings, several guys playing basketball over on the courts— boring! Then Sean saw Tim Braverton standing beside the sleek Corvette, holding a remote control unit as he maneuvered the toy car on the blacktop parking lot near where Sean had dropped his bike.

"Wow, cool," Sean thought, then impulsively bounded over to check it out. Sean was a friendly, outgoing kid who never met a stranger. He made friends easily whether at school or here at the park. His mother had given him all the usual warnings about talking to strangers, but never quite emphatic enough for the message to soak in. Sean probably wouldn't have paid attention anyway. Aside from some juvenile mischief, nothing bad ever happened in their neighborhood. He felt completely safe here at the park, even in the presence of the harmless looking stranger playing with the model car.

"That's neat," Sean said after watching Tim maneuver the car for a few minutes, itching to get his hands on the remote control. Tim didn't respond, but put the car through a series of figure 8 maneuvers to heighten Sean's interest.

"How fast does it go?" Sean asked.

"Not quite as fast as my real Vette," Tim smiled and said, "but fast enough to do a wheelie. Watch this."

Tim brought the car to a complete stop then jammed the accelerator knob forward. The remote car reared up on its back wheels and tore down the blacktop leaving a trace of smoldering rubber behind it.

"Wowee," Sean yelled as the car zipped across the parking lot like a Saturday night dragster. Just as it seemed the car would run off the blacktop, Tim eased off the accelerator, banked the car into a wide U-turn and brought it back across the blacktop at full throttle, easing it to a perfect stop right at his feet. Sean was ready to be had, Tim figured.

"Here, you want to try it?" he asked Sean as he held out the remote control.

"Wow! Can I?" Sean asked in disbelief as he timidly took the remote control half thinking that Tim was just kidding. "What do I do?"

"It's easy. Put your thumb on this button to control the speed, and steer with the knob," Tim said as he moved next to Sean. A rush of anticipation raced through him as he touched the boy and caught the scent of a kid who had been playing hard. "What joy this is going to be," he thought to himself, barely able to control his impulse to reach down and fondle Sean.

Tim stepped back and watched Sean, unsure of himself at first, slowly gain confidence in his ability to maneuver the toy car. Within minutes, however, he had completely mastered the remote control unit and soon had the car zig-zagging and spinning across the blacktop like an accomplished model car enthusiast.

"Hey, you're pretty good at this," Tim said.

Sean smiled proudly at the compliment while keeping his eye on the car zipping across the blacktop.

"It's too bad I didn't bring one of my other cars...we could race," Tim said.

"Wow, you've got another one?" Sean asked in amazement.

"Sure, we've got a whole collection of 'em...my son and I," Tim lied to get Sean to lower his guard even further. "He's out of town with his mother right now, but I don't think he'd mind if I let you race one of them."

"Cool...could we do it tomorrow," Sean replied.

"Well, I don't know...they're coming home tomorrow," Tim continued with his fabricated story. "Tell you what, though, I only live a few minutes from here. I guess I could go home and pick out a car for you and get back in plenty of time to have a race or two. You could even ride with me...in the real thing," Tim said as he motioned toward the Corvette.

"Wow, me in a Corvette," Sean replied. "But Mom told me never to get in a car with a stranger," he continued disappointedly.

"Yeah, your mother's right," Tim said. "We'd better just forget it. Maybe some other time, okay?"

Sean, who saw the opportunity slipping away, quickly replied, "I don't think she'd mind if I went with you. I mean, you've got a kid, too."

"Sure do," Tim said. "About your same age...and I've told him the same thing about strangers. Tell you what, though, my name is Tim," he said as he held out his hand to shake. "And your name is...?"

"Sean," came the reply as Tim shook his hand.

"There, now we know each other, so I'm not a stranger any more," Tim said to Sean who by now was feeling completely at ease with the situation. "Let's go get that car and get back over here while there's still plenty of light to get in some races."

Sean gathered up the toy car and smiled broadly as he slid into the leather seat of the Corvette. It would be his last smile.

***

After frantically searching the neighborhood for more than three hours, Sean's mother called the police. His abandoned bike was found at the park at 10:30 that evening. He was officially listed as a missing child the next morning. A year later, Sean's smiling face showed up on the back of a milk carton, just as thousands of other missing children's have over the years.

Long after that image had faded from our consciousness, the remains of Sean's body were found by a logging crew some 25 miles from Seattle. His was one of seven bodies of young boys discovered in the Seattle area over a four-year period.

Tim Braverton, serving a five-year sentence for sexual assault of a child, was questioned about the murders on numerous occasions, but there was insufficient evidence to link him with the crimes.

Survival Analysis

The case of Sean Matthews illustrates just how easy it is for a molester to break down the defenses of a child. Sean had been warned about the dangers of talking to adult strangers, yet in just a matter of minutes Tim Braverton was able to create enough rapport with Sean to entice him to his home. But that's not so unusual. Few children will perceive an engaging, innocent-looking stranger as a threat. Sean himself was very outgoing. He craved the companionship of others. And since his mother and father had divorced, there was a void in his life where his dad used to be. For the moment, Tim Braverton seemed like a good father substitute.

Although Sean had been warned about strangers, he had never been taught about child molesters. Some educators and even parents are reluctant to teach the dangers of child molestation and exploitation in the belief that it could frighten children to the point they become suspicious of all adults. However, it is possible to teach children about the dangers of molestation without making them paranoid. After all, we're able to teach kids about other dangers such as fire, traffic, poisons, etc., without scaring them.

Had Sean received the proper education and training, he would have known that a toy such as Tim's model car is a very common lure for child molesters. He would have immediately become suspicious when Tim suggested they leave together.

He would also have known about the importance of safety in numbers. When his friends left the park, Sean would have gone with them. A child alone is one of the easiest marks for a molester. Sean's friendly, outgoing personality made it that much easier.

Finally, had Sean been properly educated about the dangers of molestation, he might have been become suspicious when Tim suggested they go to his house. At that moment, he would have quickly moved back out of Tim's reach and would have immediately left the park. With the right training, Sean would have known exactly how to handle the situation, because he would have been well drilled in it, the same way he had been trained with fire drills.

It may seem like an extreme measure to give children abuse- and abduction-prevention drills. But at a time when more than a thousand new child abuse cases are reported daily, such drills can be critical to the safety of our kids.

How to Keep It from Happening to Your Children

1. Train your children to be aware of the dangers of molestation, sexual assault and kidnapping. However, do not use scare tactics. The idea is not to frighten your children, but to educated them. Kids should understand that most adults are committed to the welfare and protection of children.

2. Make sure your kids know how to recognize the lures used by child molesters. Some of the most common lures are:

   ASKING FOR HELP OR ASSISTANCE—This is a very common method used by molesters. The molester may ask the child for directions, or for help in finding a lost pet, or for any of a number of things. Sometimes, the molester will even pretend to be disabled or physically handicapped to get the sympathy and trust of the child.
   FAKING AUTHORITY—Some molesters go to great extremes to lure kids into their cars. They disguise themselves as everything from police officers to priests to scout

leaders. Some have even gone so far as to put flashing lights on their cars to look like police detectives.

FAKING EMERGENCIES—The molester might tell a child something like, "Your mother has been in an accident. Come with me right away." This is designed to confuse and panic the child into making a quick decision.

ATTRACTIVE ENTICEMENTS—Candy, toys and magic tricks are age-old enticements still used very effectively by today's molesters.

FRIENDSHIP AND AFFECTION—Many children are molested by someone they know and trust. They are caught off guard when someone like a relative, teacher, neighbor or family friend makes advances. Children from broken homes are particularly vulnerable to such advances.

3. Have a plan of action for your kids to follow in the case of emergencies. That way, they will know what they are supposed to do and won't be lured away by a faked emergency.

4. Teach your kids what to do if a stranger asks for assistance. Perhaps the best thing for the child to do is politely explain to the stranger that he or she should get another adult to provide assistance. All the while, however, the child should maintain a safe distance from the stranger—certainly well beyond arm's length. If the adult reaches out as if to touch or take the child's hand, the child should throw politeness to the wind and run away as fast as possible.

5. Although children must respect legitimate authority, they also should learn not to accept the trappings of that authority at face value. It is perfectly acceptable for children to politely request law enforcement officers to verify their credentials either with a call home or to the police station.

6. Teach your kids that they are never to accept gifts and favors from strangers under any circumstances. A polite but assertive refusal is the best way for kids to respond when offered such favors.

7. Children should be taught that they absolutely never get into a car with a stranger if they have even the slightest doubt about the stranger's authority.

8. From time to time, run through drills with your kids involving various scenarios. Some parents make the drill seem like a game to make it less threatening to children.

9. Get involved in "neighborhood watch" programs, and be on the lookout for strange cars cruising the neighborhood and around parks and schools. Don't be timid about reporting suspicious activities to police and/or security personnel.

10. Make sure your children have a good understanding of "private parts"—the parts of the body that are covered by a bathing suit. Children should learn that no one has the right to touch their private parts. Stress the importance of your child reporting to you if anyone tries to touch or fondle them there.

9:15 p.m., New York, New York

D on Biondi had discovered what a lot of entrepreneurs
     already knew: It's a lot easier to create a product
     than it is to market a product. Eighteen months ago,
Biondi had raised enough money to go into production with a
new toy called "Toothy Tunes," a cute little tooth-brush holder
that played music-box songs for kids as they brushed their teeth.
It was a "can't miss" product that somehow did. He had tried in
vain to market the product through toy stores, mass- merchandis-
ers and gift shops, but nothing had worked. Little more than a
thousand units had been sold; the remaining 19,000 that he had
produced were stored in a warehouse in Denver.

The investors were getting nervous. So was Biondi. He had
plowed almost his entire life savings into the venture to keep the
company operational. That's why this trip to New York was so
important. Biondi felt that the product might have a good chance
of making it as a premium item for one of the big toothpaste

manufacturers. All of those companies would be represented at the Premium and Incentive trade show in New York, so Biondi had scraped up enough money to rent a small booth there. This had to work. If it didn't, that would be the end of "Toothy Tunes," and most likely, bankruptcy for Don Biondi.

But Don Biondi had a more pressing problem on the plane trip to New York City. While he was going through a security check point at Stapleton Airport in Denver, someone had stolen his briefcase containing his wallet, his cash and all but one of his credit cards. He couldn't figure how it happened. He had placed his briefcase on the conveyor belt to be X-rayed then walked through the metal detector. The alarm went off. After emptying his pockets following the third pass through the metal detector, he finally got through. In the distraction, however, a thief had deftly walked off with his briefcase.

The only resources Biondi had with him at that point were $30 in pocket money, his return ticket and a VISA card that he had absent-mindedly tucked in his shirt pocket after using it to pay for his airline ticket at Stapleton. "Thank God I didn't put that card back in my wallet," he thought to himself as he fitfully weighed his options while picking at his dinner on the plane. He could get a cash advance from his VISA card, but he needed what little credit was left on it to pay for his hotel room. No, the only thing he could do was call his wife Gretchen when he got to New York and have her wire some money. He'd do it first thing after checking into his hotel.

It was nearly 7:30 p.m. when Don Biondi arrived at his hotel on the Avenue of the Americas near Times Square. The cab fare and tip had eaten up 28 of his 30 dollars. The last time he was in New York, he thought he remembered cab fare being about $12 from Kennedy Airport. He was sure the driver had ripped him off, but he paid the fare without complaint. So far, it had been a lousy trip. And it was about to get a lot worse.

Biondi presented his credit card at the hotel registration desk. When the clerk ran it through for authorization, the card was refused. Apparently he was over his limit. He explained his situation to the desk clerk. The clerk, who had evidently heard every story in the book, was unmoved. His only option, he was told, was to pay cash in advance. And if he couldn't pay by 9:00, he would lose his reservation. Biondi demanded to talk to the manager. The night manager rudely told him the same thing. No credit, no cash, no room. End of conversation.

Biondi went to a pay phone in the lobby and placed a collect call to Gretchen. It was still 5:30 in Denver, time for Gretchen to get to the bank, get money and wire it to him. An hour later, he called Gretchen back. She had managed to scrape up $500 and had taken it to Western Union. The money had been wired to a Western Union office on Broadway, about 10 blocks from his hotel. The two dollars in his pocket would barely buy a cup of coffee in New York City, let alone a cab ride. He would have to walk.

By now, it was nearly 9:00 p.m. in New York, and the animals around Times Square had come out of their dens. If ever there was a more vivid example of decadence in America, Biondi hadn't seen it. Pimps, pushers, hookers and hawkers of X-rated entertainment scurried around Times Square like rats at a garbage dump. Empty-eyed derelicts wandered from trash can to trash can, foraging for scraps of food or aluminum cans. A dangerous-looking man wearing a cape and a cowboy hat walked by and asked for a cigarette. Biondi didn't reply but kept on walking. The man shouted something at him; Biondi pretended not to hear. "Don't stop, don't talk, just keep walking," Biondi told himself.

"Just get the money, get back to the hotel, and get some sleep," he muttered as he walked past another man muttering to himself. "What a freak show," he thought.

Vick and Sonny Feligno, keeping their nightly vigil across the street from the Western Union office on Broadway, saw Don Biondi go inside. The office was well-lighted, so they had no trouble seeing Biondi take the cash from the clerk behind the bullet-proof glass cage, count it and put it in his right front pants pocket. Vick and Sonny had the routine down perfectly. They laid in wait for their unsuspecting victims to leave the Western Union office, always with cash. Don Biondi would be easy prey. At least, he should have been.

Biondi didn't notice Vick crossing Broadway and falling in behind him. Or Sonny paralleling him across the street. There were hundreds of people on the street. Just as Biondi was approaching 29th and Broadway, he heard someone behind him say, "Excuse me, sir," and felt a hand on his shoulder. He wheeled around. There was Vick holding up a wallet with a fake police badge.

"I'm a police officer," Vick said as he took Biondi's arm. "Would you step over here please."

"What for?" Biondi said as he tried to decide whether to comply or pull away.

"Just step over here. We need to speak to you," Vick replied just as Sonny walked up.

"Is this the guy?" Sonny asked as part of the scam.

"He sure looks like him," Vick replied as the stepped into the dimly lit doorway of a closed store on 29th Street just off Broadway.

"Hey, look, I haven't done anything. I'm just on my way back to my hotel," Biondi protested.

"Yeah, and you didn't sell any drugs back there, huh?" Vick replied sarcastically.

"No, I didn't!" Biondi said emphatically.

"Well, let's just see. Turn around and spread 'em," Vick said as Sonny stood lookout.

"What...you've got to be kidding," Biondi replied incredulously.

At that, Sonny pulled out a revolver and shoved it in Biondi's stomach. "We ain't kiddin' asshole. Turn around and spread 'em," Vick commanded as he roughly whirled Biondi around and forced him to lean forward with his palms against the glass window of the store.

He patted Biondi's pants pocket and felt the lump of cash. "Well, well, whatta we have here," Vick said as he pulled the roll of bills out of Biondi's pocket.

"I just got that from Western Union," Biondi said through a quivering voice.

"Yeah, and I got this at Bloomingdales," Vick laughed sarcastically as he stuck the gun under Biondi's nose. "Here, hold this for evidence," Vick said as he handed Sonny the money.

"Yeah, I'll do that," Sonny said. At that, both men bolted and ran, playing dodge the car as they zig-zagged across Broadway. Biondi looked around, knowing he'd been suckered.

"You son-of-a-bitch!" Biondi screamed as he started to run after them, paying no attention whatever to the "Don't Walk" signal flashing at the corner of 29th and Broadway. He had his sight set on Vick and Sonny a half a block up 29th, and he didn't want to lose sight of them. He didn't see the cab racing north up Broadway trying to beat the light. The driver didn't even have time to hit the brake before the cab struck Biondi, sending him flying up and over the speeding cab. He landed head first on the pavement.

Vick and Sonny never looked back, never knew what had happened to Don Biondi. The next night, they were back on Broadway to put on their show for another victim.

Don Biondi's death was ruled an accident. "Toothy Tunes" died a merciful death at the hands of a bankruptcy judge.

Survival Analysis

Although Don Biondi was a desperate man, his reaction was irrational at best. Chasing armed robbers through a busy street, particularly, for someone who is unarmed, is not the best course of action. What would Biondi have done in the unlikely event he was able to catch them. He could easily have been killed by one of the gunmen. Instead, he was killed by a speeding cab. Giving chase was certainly the worst of Don Biondi's mistakes. But not the only one.

Biondi's problems really began at Stapleton Airport in Denver. He should never have been carrying his wallet in his briefcase, especially in an airport where he had to let it leave his hands to get through the security checkpoint. Security check-points are some of the least secure areas for bags and purses, especially for someone who is detained at the metal detector. It's easy for a thief to quickly pick up a briefcase or bag and make off with it.

Also, Biondi shouldn't have been carrying everything in cash. Had he been carrying travelers' checks, it would have been a simple procedure to have them replaced. Some travelers' check companies will even deliver replacement checks to you.

When Biondi picked up his cash at Western Union in New York, he made the mistake of leaving the office on foot. With cash in his pocket, he could have hailed a cab right in front of the office. He already felt uncomfortable in the area, so it's surprising that he decided to walk back to the hotel.

The situation with Vick and Sonny is a difficult one to correctly call. It's hard to tell plain clothes police officers from the criminals they're trying to infiltrate. However, fake police badges are a dime a dozen. Biondi would have been within his rights to ask to see some identification besides the badge. When they refused to show him other identification, he might have suspected they were imposters. At that point, it would have been appropriate to scream for help.

When Vick pulled the revolver, however, Biondi could do nothing but comply. Whether Biondi suspected they were phonies made no difference at that point. He was right to give up his money, especially with the gun stuck in his stomach. When Vick and Sonny turned and ran, he should have been thankful he was still alive. Sure, the robbers had his money, but he had survived the incident. As desperately as he needed the cash, it wasn't worth risking death to get it back.

About the most he could have accomplished under the circumstances was to note as much as possible about the assailants' physical appearance. When he reported the incident to police, he would have been able to give the police a good description. Although it's a long shot, the police might have been able to make an arrest and possibly retrieve the stolen money.

How to Keep It from Happening to You

1. Do not carry cash, credit cards, airline tickets or passports in a purse or briefcase. Carry them in a neck pouch instead (a pouch on a cord that slips around your neck inside your shirt or blouse). Belt pouches also can be used, but they are not as secure as a neck pouch. Never carry large amounts of cash if you can avoid it. Use travelers checks instead.

2. When you go through security checkpoints at airports, keep your eyes on your purse and carry-on luggage at all times. You will lose sight of it briefly as it goes through the X-ray unit, but try to be there waiting for it when it comes through.

3. If you get stopped at the metal detector walkway, ask the guard to retrieve your purse or bag before he or she proceeds to check the contents on your person. Leaving purses, packages or bags unattended while you are detained and searched places them at great risk of being stolen. It only takes an instant for a thief to grab your bags and go, especially in a security-check area where there's a lot of rushing and confusion.

4. Don't leave your bags unattended at airports for any reason. It's not uncommon to see unattended bags at curbside drop-off points, in waiting areas, outside restroom stalls or in airport snack bars and cafeterias. Remember, though, thieves routinely work airports waiting for someone to leave bags or possessions unattended. Thieves arouse no suspicion at all in picking up a bag and walking off with it.

5. When your plane reaches its destination, proceed directly to the baggage claim area in an effort to be there before your luggage arrives. Even in airports where claim checks are required, it's easy for a thief to make off with luggage in the confusion

6. If at all possible, put a lock on all carry-on bags and keep them locked at all times. Use any kind of locking device your purse might have as well. At the very least, keep your purse zipped tightly shut.

7. Never sleep in airport waiting rooms unless you're traveling with a companion who is awake to watch your valuables. If you fall asleep on the plane, rest your feet on your bag under the seat in front of you; if someone tries to remove or open your bags, they will have to move your feet to do it.

8. Try to keep your purse in your lap as often as possible. Avoid putting your purse beneath the seat in front of you unless it's absolutely necessary. Never leave your wallet or airline tickets in a purse or coat pocket you store in an overhead compartment.

9. When you are in a strange city, try to determine the safety of an area before you go into it, especially if you are on foot.

10. Never try to resist an armed assailant. It is better to comply than to die.

10:25 p.m., St. Louis, Missouri

T he cool front had brought some much needed rain. But that didn't matter to Sandy Malugen. She cursed it as she inched along with the traffic on Loop 270 in St. Louis. "People just don't know how to drive in the rain," she always said. "The first thing they do is hit the brake pedal at the first sign of moisture."

Traffic on the Loop was at a virtual standstill due to an overturned 18-wheeler that had jackknifed on the wet road and smashed into three cars, killing two of the occupants. Police, fire, ambulance and wrecker crews further complicated the scene by blocking the only lane not directly involved in the accident.

Sandy Malugen was already mad when she stopped her car at the end of a river of taillights stalled in front of her. She slammed open palms against the steering wheel, then jacked up the volume on the stereo out of frustration. She laid her head back on the headrest to try to calm herself. The wipers sweeping the rain from the windshield had a hypnotic effect on Sandy as she thought back to what had occurred at dinner less than an hour ago.

Jay Toney, her fiancee, had told her over dinner that he wanted to postpone their wedding, scheduled for three weeks hence. When asked why, Jay merely looked down at his veal and shrugged. Sandy was normally very easy-going and difficult to anger. However, once angered, she became consumed by its fire and it generally took days for it to burn itself out. She flew into a rage at her fiance's suggestion. All the arrangements for the wedding had been made, and the invitations were ready to go in the mail. Too angry even to speak, she stormed out of the restaurant leaving Jay sitting there in amazement.

Now this! God, she hated this city.

Then a horn honking from behind her snapped her out of her reverie. She looked up and saw that the cars in front of her had pulled up about ten feet. The fact that the driver behind her had honked only exacerbated her anger.

"Up yours, jerk off," she screamed as she impulsively shot him the finger, not knowing whether he could see it through the rain drenched rear window. She hoped he saw it, though. The fact that she didn't inch along in the traffic fast enough to suit the butt-head behind her was just too damn bad.

The traffic in the lane to her left started slowly moving forward. Sandy put on her left blinker and hoped that some kind-hearted person would let her move into that lane. The car behind her, the one that had just honked at her, flashed his lights at her. Thinking the driver was going to move left and then let her move over in front invoked a courteous wave from Sandy.

It took Sandy another ten minutes to work her way up past the accident scene. She doggedly kept from looking over at the accident. She hated rubber-neckers who slowed down to ogle traffic accidents. Once past the accident scene, Sandy gunned the engine and sped away. She was surprised to see another car right behind her with the driver flashing his lights at her.

"No way, Jose. I'm not stopping or pulling over tonight," she said as she glanced in her rear view mirror. She wondered if it was the car she had angrily gestured at.

Sandy took the next exit off the freeway and then turned right at an intersection. The car was right behind her, following dangerously close. She felt a twinge of fear mixed with anger. She made a left onto her street. The other car followed.

"Get off my ass, butthole!" she shouted at the unseen driver. Sandy accelerated, trying to put some distance between them, but the other car stayed with her. "The hell with it," she screamed, then gestured angrily. For some reason, the other car backed off. When Sandy checked her rear-view mirror a moment later, the car was nowhere to be seen.

As she continued on, she passed a convenience store with a police car parked out front. Sandy thought about stopping to tell the police about the threatening actions of the tailgater. By now, though, the car was nowhere to be seen, and it was raining harder, so she decided to drive on. It was times like these that she wished she had a car phone, though. The driver of the car seemed really angry. She knew it was dumb to provoke another driver, but he was being a real jerk. No harm done, though. Apparently, the car had turned off somewhere behind her.

Benny Tolliver fingered the trigger of the nine millimeter semi- automatic pistol in his lap. He was 200 feet behind the car and the bitch driving it. He had turned off his headlights and continued following her. Benny saw the police car at the convenience store, too. He started to turn his lights back on. He didn't want to get pulled over before he got even with the bitch who had shot him the finger. He was going to teach her a lesson she'd never forget.

Sandy slowed down and turned into the driveway of her apartment complex. To get into the parking area, she had to stop at the security gate and open it with her access card. She had to fumble around in her purse to find the access card. She couldn't see in the darkness, so she turned on the inside light. She finally located the card and hit the button to lower the car window.

Just as she was about to insert the card in the slot, she saw Benny Tolliver. He seemed to come out of nowhere.

"You like shooting the finger, huh, bitch," Benny said through clenched teeth.

Sandy immediately realized who the man was. "I'm calling the cops if you don't get out of here right now," Sandy said as she inserted the access card in the slot.

"You like shooting the finger, I like shooting this," Benny said as he levelled the pistol at her face.

"Oh, God, please don't," Sandy screamed as she saw the gun.

The access card tripped a mechanism and the apartment gate started to open. At the same moment, Benny opened fire. All six bullets tore into Sandy's face and neck, killing her instantly. Her foot on the brake relaxed and her car powered forward, crashing into a parked car just inside the gate. Benny Tolliver ran to his car and sped away. There were no witnesses to the shooting, and Benny Tolliver was never arrested.

Survival Analysis

Sandy Malugen let her anger get the better of her, and she paid for it with her life. In the age of crime, many Americans have started carrying handguns for personal protection, even though it's illegal to do so in most states. But a handgun carried for defense can just as easily become an offensive weapon during a heated argument. Even innocent confrontations between motorists have turned deadly as one or more of the parties pulled out a gun and started shooting.

Sandy would most likely be alive today if she hadn't gestured contemptuously to the car behind her. Her death is a classic example of how easy it is to get killed these days. It's indicative of a society with some very sick members.

In recent years, the incidence of a driver pulling a gun and firing at another motorist has become almost as commonplace as rush hour traffic. Bearing in mind that many motorists are armed and maybe dangerous, the best advice we can offer is this: avoid ANY confrontation with another motorist, no matter how slight.

If you happen to do something that angers another driver, don't aggravate the situation further with gestures, words or glares. Sandy Malugen gestured not once, but twice. She also waved her hand which her killer may have mistaken for another angry gesture. In effect, she turned something as insignificant as a horn honk into a contest that turned bloody.

Sandy still might have survived the encounter had she followed her basic instincts. She thought the angry driver still might be following her, yet she drove past the police car parked in front of the convenience store. Had Benny seen her talking to the police, that might have scared him away and the incident would have ended then and there.

Although Sandy initiated the encounter by making gestures, she is not to blame for her death. The blame rests squarely on Benny Tolliver. But Sandy's death does underscore the importance of playing it safe with other motorists. You never know when the person in the car behind you is another Benny Tolliver. Something else to bear in mind. As statistics bear out, there are a lot of people on the road driving under the influence of drugs or alcohol. Their judgement is naturally impaired, and under certain conditions, they might do something they wouldn't ordinarily do, especially if they have a gun handy. You certainly don't want to deal with a drunk in a car with a gun.

Your best bet in traffic: stay calm and in control, drive courteously, obey traffic laws—and don't let your emotions get in the way of common sense. You won't lose anything in avoiding conflicts with other motorists. You could possibly save your life.

How to Keep It from Happening to You

1. Drive courteously and obey traffic laws. Try to stay calm and in control of your emotions.

2. Never shout or gesture angrily at another motorist.

3. Use your horn only as a warning device, not as a way to blow off steam at the actions of another motorist. If you have to honk at another car, avoid making eye contact with the driver or its occupants.

4. Never stop your car and get out to encounter another motorist, unless, of course, your car is involved in an accident. Be cautious even then. Gangs that stage accidents either to rob the driver or steal the car operate all across the country.

5. Never turn an encounter in traffic into a test of will or a
    matter of principle. Remember, some motorists have been
    drinking; alcohol is a depressant that can heighten anger and
    aggression. Remember, too, that many motorists are armed
    and potentially dangerous—especially in the heat of anger.

11:55 p.m., Chicago, Illinois

Helen Stanton walked into the club and felt that secret tingle as all eyes riveted on her. She was incredibly beautiful, and she knew it. She could have any guy in here at the bat of an eye. Maybe she'd let some guy get lucky tonight. Then again, maybe she wouldn't. She wasn't looking for just any encounter. Tonight, she had something very special in mind.

Helen knew all the caveats of the singles bar scene, but frankly, she was fed up with all that crap. She was young and single, and damned if she wasn't going to enjoy herself. All she ever heard was "don't, don't, don't" at a time when she wanted to do, do, do. Sex was one of the most important things in her life, and she had deluded herself into thinking that if she protected herself, promiscuity was not only acceptable, it was downright fun. The delicious thrill of sex with a total stranger had become like a drug to her. She was hooked. And like a junkie looking for a new drug, Helen's addiction pushed her closer and closer to the edge in quest of a better high. The minute Helen spied Les Monroe, she knew she had found it.

Les was seated at the bar on the other side of the dance floor when he saw Helen make her entrance. He watched her brush past a group of young lions in power ties and take the only empty seat at the bar, a few seats down from his. It was as if the seat had been reserved for her.

Les swiveled on his stool to get a view of Helen in the mirror behind the bar. His icy glare caught her eye, and she smiled ever so slightly. Every guy in this place was intimidated by her five-foot eight-inch stature and the confidence exuded from her deep brown eyes. Every guy except Les, that is. And Helen could sense it. She felt a rush of excitement as their eyes met. God, they were cold, she thought. Unfeeling, uncaring, scary in a sense.

Uncharacteristically, she looked away. "Gin and tonic," she replied as the bar tender asked her pleasure. She lit a cigarette and batted a quick glance at Les in the mirror. He stared right through her. "Damn, this guy is like ice," Helen thought to herself. The challenge was to make him melt. Helen knew she was up to it. That was her first mistake.

Les Monroe was a hunter, soon to be a killer. He, too, played the singles club game, but he played it out of loathing rather than lust. Les usually would hang around one club or another watching the women come and go, but never with him. In fact, Les had never once been successful in picking up a woman in a club. He hated them for the rejection, and he secretly dreamed of the day he'd get his revenge. His wait was just about over.

As a teen-ager, Les had been fascinated with cases involving serial murders. He closely followed the case of the Hillside Murders in Los Angeles, as well as the case of Ted Bundy in

Washington and Florida. He was actually outraged when Bundy was convicted and put to death in Florida. Several year ago, Les had begun fantasizing about murder, about how it must feel to kill anonymously, at random, and leave the police without a clue. More recently, he had formulated a plan. All he needed was the right circumstance, and he was convinced he would do it.

But finding a victim hadn't been easy for Les. While he was physically attractive enough, his personality had scared away numerous women he had targeted in clubs. Why he continually trolled singles bars was a mystery even to Les. It only fueled his anger and frustration. Although, he had identified it as the best way to find a single, unattached female who might be inclined to fall into his trap, he had never come close in more than five months of trying. To snare someone as attractive as Helen was beyond his wildest imagination.

"What a bitch," he thought to himself as he watched Helen in the mirror. "She's teasing me with this little game. I'd like to bust her cute little head open...after I make her feel a little pain first...no, a lot of pain...she might even like it...no, no way she'd like the pain. I'd like to give it to her good, though," Les' thoughts rambled as he watched Helen suck provocatively on the straw in her glass.

Then Helen turned up the heat a notch as she held her drink glass in both hands and went down on the straw without taking her eyes off Les. The implication was obvious, and Helen fully expected Les to make his move on her. But he just sat there with his seemingly insouciant stare, concealing the anger churning inside. As much as he wanted to respond, he couldn't bring himself to move. She would not only reject him, he thought, she'd probably laugh right in his face. And everybody in the bar would see it.

"Damn, this guy is a stone," Helen thought to herself. "I must be losing it...no, no way I'm losing it...he just doesn't have a spine...guess I'll just have to take over...might be kind of fun molding this lump of putty...probably a virgin...I've gotta have this guy."

Helen paid for her drink, and casually walked up to Les. "Are you going to sit there all night dreaming about it, or do you want to make it happen?" she asked.

At first, Les was too startled to reply. The trace of a grin appeared on his lips and he said half joking, "I'm ready any time you are."

She moved closer to him and whispered, "You better be good and ready...because, baby, you're about to get the ride of your life. I'm going to the ladies' room...I'll meet you outside," she said as she turned to leave.

Les was shaking slightly as he fumbled in his pocket for money to pay his tab, still not sure whether Helen was serious or just playing with his head. He stepped out into the cool Chicago night, and waited for several minutes. As usual, State Street was teeming with young people playing out the rituals of the singles bar culture. He looked at his watch impatiently. "Damn, that bitch is in there laughing her head off," he muttered to himself as he paced nervously in front of the door. Fury was welling up inside him. Thoughts of his fist smashing into her face ran through his head.

He turned and walked partway down the block, cursing and damning Helen like a sidewalk preacher. Then, in his agitation, he turned and headed back toward the bar. "I'll fix that teasing piece of shit," he said to himself as he approached the door. Just as he was reaching for the door, it opened from the inside, and Helen stepped out.

"I thought you'd have a cab waiting," she snapped.

"We don't need a cab. My place is just a few blocks away," he replied. "You ready?"

"I'm always ready. I just hope you are," she said as they turned to go.

Les Monroe felt a twinge of uncertainty as he nervously fumbled with the key in the lock of his apartment door. All the thinking and planning and waiting for the right opportunity was about to pay off it seemed, but now he wasn't sure he could carry it out. He had never killed before. Could he really do it? Of course he could. He had found the perfect victim, and no one had even seen them leave the bar together.

"I hope this isn't an indication of your ability to hit the hole, lover," Helen chided as Les fumbled with the keyhole in the semi-darkness outside the door of his brownstone two blocks off State Street. "I'll hit the hole all right, bitch," Les thought to himself. "We'll see if you're still so high and mighty after I get through with you," he thought as he finally found the key hole and opened the door. He stepped inside and turned on the light.

Helen breezed past him and glanced around the fashionably decorated town house. "You must be rich," she said as she tossed her coat onto the couch and began removing her blouse.

Les watched her undress without speaking. Fewer than fifty words had passed between them—in fact, neither knew the other's name—and here was this beautiful stranger standing naked in the middle of his living room. Les couldn't believe his eyes. Or his good fortune. He couldn't have found a more perfect victim. Beautiful, brimming with self confidence—and a total bitch. God, if anybody deserved what was about to happen it was this bitch, Les thought to himself as he stood there still wearing his coat and gloves.

"Well, are you going to stand there gawking or are you going to take your clothes off?" Helen asked as she slowly moved toward him. She pressed herself against his fully clothed body, then felt a hot rush of excitement as he roughly grabbed her buttock with his gloved hand. He slowly traced a line with his finger to her shoulder and then to her neck. The leather gloves somehow added to Helen's passion. Les brought his other hand up in what Helen thought was to be an embrace.

Suddenly, though, both hands were pressed around her neck, with thumbs forced against her windpipe. Les saw the surprise and fear in her eyes as she instinctively brought her hands up in an attempt to break the hold on her throat. She tried to scream, but nothing came but gasps for air and a painful gurgling moan. The look of shock and horror Les saw on her face would be permanently imprinted in his mind like a snapshot. The power and control he felt at that moment was beyond measure.

Helen made a vain attempt to bring her knee up into Les' groin, but all it did was cause her to lose her balance and fall backward and to the left. Les was right on top of her as she fell. He brought his knees up in kneeling position over her chest while maintaining the grip on her throat. He squeezed harder as her struggling subsided.

He continued to choke her for more than five minutes. Gradually, cautiously, Les began to relax the hold on her neck. He rolled off her lifeless body and lay there for a few moments. He realized he was breathing heavily and sweating profusely. He turned his head to look at her. He was surprised at how peaceful she seemed, almost like a lover basking in the blissful sleep of afterglow.

After a few minutes, Les went to a closet where he had been storing a large heavy-gauge plastic drop cloth. He laid it out on the floor, placed Helen's body on on top, and carefully rolled her up inside. Then he picked her up and made his way to the basement where her coffin was waiting—a large door-top freezer, empty and unused until now.

Les had bought the freezer five months ago as part of his macabre plan. He had set the temperature at the lowest setting in anticipation of what he planned to keep inside. When Les swung open the door of the freezer, the frigid air inside hit him in the face like a Chicago winter. "This ought to hold you for a while," he thought as he lowered Helen's plastic-wrapped body inside.

He closed the door on the freezer and went upstairs to gather up Helen's clothing. The smell of her perfume still lingered on her blouse. He pressed it to his face and inhaled deeply. He then disrobed and masturbated while fantasizing about Helen. It was the greatest sex he had ever had.

Nearly a year later, on April Fool's Day, Les would remove Helen's nude body from the freezer and dump it in Washington Park. By the time the body was discovered nearly 18 hours later, it had completely thawed from its frozen state. Since it had been kept in almost suspended animation for more than 11 months, forensics experts were unable to pinpoint an exact time of death.

Les Monroe gleefully read the accounts of the case in the newspaper. This was one murder the cops would never solve, he thought to himself. The thrill of it all made him heighten his search for a second victim. Come next April Fool's Day, there had to be another body and a baffling case for the police.

Three weeks later, Les would find his second victim. Meanwhile, police are still searching for clues in the death of Helen Stanton.

Survival Analysis

Some people might argue that Helen Stanton deserved little sympathy. After all, she knew the dangers of her behavior, but acted anyway. We couldn't disagree more. Helen Stanton's only fault was in being human. She had a powerful sex drive that needed to be fulfilled in ways that seem bizarre to most people.

No matter how strange, or even perverse, her behavior might seem, the fact remains that Helen Stanton should never be blamed for what happened to her that night in Chicago. The blame rests squarely on the shoulders of Les Monroe, whose need was so sick and twisted that it took Helen's life—and may yet take others.

The fact that Les Monroe and thousands of others like him are walking the streets should be a warning to every one. But a lot of people won't take heed. Every night, in big city clubs and small town bars alike, similar scenarios are being acted out. We certainly don't condone such behavior. In fact, we strongly advise against it.

However, even as Helen persisted in her reckless behavior, she might have survived the encounter by doing a few things differently. For one thing, she should never have gone it alone. Before she left the bar with Les, she should have gotten his name and address and told a friend or acquaintance that she was leaving with Les. She should have made certain that Les was aware that another person knew she was leaving with him. That might have deterred Les. After all, his plan turned on anonymity.

Once they arrived at Les' apartment, the very first thing Helen should have done was to call a friend to advise of her whereabouts and the time she expected to be back home. This, too, might have kept Les from following through with his plan for murder.

Although we're not strong advocates of self-defense training for most people, we would highly recommend it for people with life-styles similar to Helen's. Had she known something about self-defense, she might have been able to break the choke-hold Les had on her. A punch to the Adam's apple, thumbs jammed forcefully in the eye sockets, a simultaneous blow to both ears—anyone of them might have incapacitated Les long enough for Helen to break the hold and possibly escape.

It goes without saying that the safest thing Helen could have done was not to have left with a stranger. But people being the creatures they are—particularly young people with a feeling of immortality—often turn a deaf ear to the warnings about strangers.

It's a sad commentary on our society, but we have to keep our guard up around strangers at all times, regardless of the circumstances or surroundings.

How to Keep It from Happening to You

1. Never forget that there are sick-minded killers living in our midst, many of whom look and act perfectly normal. Any time you leave with a stranger, you could be placing yourself in great danger.

2. ALWAYS use the buddy system so someone will know where you are and what time you'll be back home.

3. If you can't or won't alter your life-style, learn self-defense to give yourself at least a fighting chance if you're attacked.

4. If you do learn self-defense, don't let it lull you into a false sense of security. Your assailant may be stronger, more

experienced or even armed with a weapon. Once an assailant is close enough to touch you, you're in danger of being overpowered. The best defense is to avoid getting in situations where you're vulnerable to attack.

5. Carry a strong, dependable chemical spray as an extra measure of defense. We recommend The Protector, a military-grade chemical protection that will stop an assailant from up to 15 feet away. The Protector is available in a purse-size canister that attaches to a key chain, which can easily be held in the palm of the hand. Even with a spray like The Protector, however, don't let it give you a false sense of security. Remember, the best defense is to avoid dangerous situations altogether.